teen's

guides

LIVING
with
EATING
DISORDERS

Also in the
Teen's Guides series

teen's guides

LIVING
with
EATING
DISORDERS

Sheila A. Cooperman, M.D.
with Sara Dulaney Gilbert

Facts On File
An imprint of Infobase Publishing

Living with Eating Disorders

Copyright © 2009 by Sheila A. Cooperman, M.D.

Facts On File, Inc.
An imprint of Infobase Publishing, Inc.
132 West 31st Street
New York NY 10001

Library of Congress Cataloging-in-Publication Data
Cooperman, Sheila.
  Living with eating disorders / Sheila Cooperman.
      p. cm. — (Teen's guides)
  Includes bibliographical references and index.
  ISBN-13: 978-0-8160-7328-3 (hardcover : alk. paper)
  ISBN-10: 0-8160-7328-7 (hardcover : alk. paper)
  1. Eating disorders in adolescence—Juvenile literature. I. Title.
  RJ506.E18C664   2009
  618.92′8526—dc22   2008028248

Facts On File books are available at special discounts when purchased in bulk quantities for businesses, associations, institutions, or sales promotions. Please call our Special Sales Department in New York at (212) 967-8800 or (800) 322-8755.

You can find Facts On File on the World Wide Web at http://www.factsonfile.com

Text design by Annie O'Donnell
Cover design by Jooyoung An

Printed in the United States of America

Bang Hermitage 10 9 8 7 6 5 4 3 2 1

This book is printed on acid-free paper.

CONTENTS

What Is an Eating Disorder?

At age 12, Andrea felt that her life would be perfect if only she were more slender. Life was pretty confusing right now: She sometimes didn't even know who she was, and her family seemed to be always in turmoil. Her parents were fighting a lot and her brother had just left for the army. Plus, middle school was so much harder than last year, and her best friends had gone to other schools. All of a sudden everything seemed to be about her "future": she was expected to get good grades, be a good athlete, and always look "nice." Even her body seemed to be turning against her—sometimes she just felt creepy in her own skin! To make things better, Andrea tried to do everything right, but she couldn't always be perfect—and that made her miserable. Her one escape was into the fantastic celebrity world on Web sites, TV, and her favorite magazines. Her favorite personalities looked so happy there. Their lives looked perfect—and they were so thin! So Andrea started a diet.

Trouble was, Andrea wasn't really fat—she just "felt" fat. She also felt that, with so many aspects of her life out of control, one thing she could control was her eating. But once she started the diet, she couldn't stop. She never seemed to look thin enough in the mirror, no matter how much she starved herself. Andrea has a kind of eating disorder called *anorexia nervosa,* one of a number of common *eating disorders* you'll learn about in this book, in addition to *bulimia nervosa, binge eating,* and obsessive exercise (*athletica nervosa*).

In recent years, eating disorders (including the awareness that they are about much more than food) have received widespread attention, and that should make dealing with them easier than it was a few generations ago. But that positive turn toward prevention and treatment can also add to the confusion about these serious illnesses. For instance, when people approach adolescence, their eating patterns may well change, with tastes shifting and intake increasing. As a teen or preteen, your body is changing shape, too. Girls often gain weight around age 10 or 11 (boys a bit later) in preparation for a growth spurt, and kids may seem to sprout like bean vines overnight.

Sometimes people mistakenly apply labels—"fat" or "anorexic"—to what is normal development. Only a small percentage of teens actually develop true eating disorders, but those who do can be in real danger. Families may not want to admit the danger, or they may overlook real problems with a "they'll grow out of it" attitude.

In addition, while all that physical change is going on, young people are bombarded with a lot of misleading visual images and misinformation in the media about what the "perfect" body is and how to achieve it. Studies reported by the National Eating Disorders Association show that 40 percent of girls under 10 say they want to "be thinner," with twice that number saying they're afraid of "getting fat."

Often a serious eating disorder can begin with something as simple as a person being unhappy with the way his or her body looks in the mirror, or with trying a diet that is "guaranteed to succeed." These disorders usually include a need to keep them secret, so they are often hidden until they have become serious.

Though such illnesses can be dangerous and even fatal, they are treatable, so understanding them matters a lot. The first important step toward living healthily with eating disorders—in a friend, a family member, or yourself—is to understand what they are, and what they're not.

WHAT ARE EATING DISORDERS?

Do you know anyone like Andrea—someone who never seems to eat and keeps getting thinner? Or maybe someone who spends many hours daily in the gym? Or who disappears after meals? Or who has simply become obsessed with being "perfect"? Not everyone who is careful about food, or who starts an exercise program, has a disorder. A new awareness about their bodies can inspire teens to healthy actions that don't necessarily lead to problems. But Andrea is a typical example of someone likely to develop an eating disorder. Risk factors include age and specific triggers—events and conditions that may precipitate eating disorders.

Some 90 percent of those afflicted with eating disorders are adolescent and young adult women. More than 1 million American teenagers and preteens live with an eating disorder—about 3 percent of that population. While it's mostly girls and young women who suffer either anorexia, bulimia, or binge eating, these serious and potentially fatal disorders now affect children as young as nine and, increasingly, boys and men as well.

Change and stress are difficult to cope with, and teens experience a great deal of change and stress in their daily lives. Some have more difficulty than others, and eating disorders may be triggered. For example, Andrea's environment is disordered, and the only thing she can fully control is her food intake. She is surrounded by messages that say "slim means happy," and she feels she has to be "perfect" to be accepted in her world. So she makes the decision that she has to lose weight. (Learning to make decisions on their own is a big part of teens' development, but sometimes they base their decisions on wrong information.)

Look at the examples in the sidebar, "What Do You Think?" Do any of them make you think about yourself? Or ask yourself this: When you look in the mirror, are you always happy with what you see? Many teens are not, because they are having to get used to a "new" body. But before they start in on a "magic" diet, they need some important facts.

It's easy to see why it might be especially hard to identify eating disorders in people your age. Teens may have eating patterns—eating constantly it seems, or never—which parents wish were different. True eating disorders go well beyond this: they are medically and psychiatrically recognized illnesses, complex conditions involving mental, physical, and social issues.

If there is confusion about food-related problems, that is not surprising. Although there are reports of conditions like anorexia and bulimia from many centuries in the past, psychiatric and medical researchers began to study them seriously only a few decades ago. Scientific knowledge about them began growing rapidly around the turn of the 21st century, with new brain-research techniques. Today eating disorders have quite specific definitions.

According to the National Institute of Mental Health, eating disorders involve serious disturbances in eating behavior, such as extreme and unhealthy reduction of food intake or severe overeating, as well as feelings of distress or extreme concern about body shape or weight.

(continues on page 6)

What Do You Think?

Which teens seem the most likely candidates for an eating disorder?

1. Mary, who wants to lose weight to fit into a prom dress.

2. Lester, whose parents are both overweight.

3. Alf, who exercises four hours a day.

4. Sonya, who always has to wear the latest style in tiny sizes, but who eats a lot.

5. Sally, who is getting skinnier and skinnier, but telling everyone that she's fine.

6. Stan, who has been a picky eater since he was a baby.

7. Angelina, whose dream is to be a ballet dancer.

8. Laura, who already smokes a pack of cigarettes a day.

Actually, all of the above might be affected by eating disorders, but each in a different way. You'll find detailed explanations and explorations of the facts throughout this book, but here are the short answers:

1. If Mary's diet stops when she can wear the dress—and if she's *dieting* to make her outer self look as good as her inner self feels—then she may be okay. But researchers note that many eating disorders begin with a diet, especially when that diet is intended to "fix" a person's sense of inadequacy.

2. Though there's some evidence of genetic connections in eating disorders, Lester won't necessarily inherit his parents' obesity. But if Lester's parents' weight issues have emotional causes, they might not be able to give Lester sufficient emotional support. One theory of eating disorders is that they are designed to "fill up" emotional emptiness.

3. Wanting to exercise is a healthy impulse for teens concerned with "looking good." But four hours a day is excessive; Alf may be already in the grips of the eating disorder called exercise obsession, or *athletica nervosa*.

4. If Sonya's head is always in the fashion magazines and Web sites, she is being bombarded with images of impossibly skinny models as ideals. She may be eating a lot, but she may also be "purging" or getting rid of the food to keep her weight down. While she may have bulimia, she might just be slender and fashionable by nature.

5. Sally may seem the most obvious eating-disorder "type": getting skinnier and skinnier, but telling everyone that she's fine, can fit the anorexia model, especially if she experiences other common psychological or social factors. Secrecy is a big part of the eating-disorder pattern: Some teens can hide them from their families for months. But it's also possible she has some other disorder that is keeping her from gaining weight, or she may just be in a growth spurt that uses up a lot of calories. Better to turn to a professional for an accurate diagnosis.

6. Some kids, like Stan, carry eating habits that began when they were very young. A picky eater since childhood may just have supersensitive taste buds and may become a gourmet. But if the early eating issues are expressions of psychological conflicts, they may later develop into disordered eating patterns.

7. Teens like Angelina, whose dream is to be a ballet dancer, may be more prone to eating disorders because their lifestyle-goal demands slimness. Likewise, someone whose goal is to be a star athlete is more likely than a bookworm to develop an exercise obsession. Not all dancers, athletes, entertainment stars, or models have eating disorders, of course, but surveys indicate that these kinds of professions have more than others.

8. The smoking of cigarettes at a young age, as in Laura's case, can indicate an overconcern with weight, since nicotine is thought to suppress appetite. Whether that's the motivation or not, nicotine is an addictive drug, and doctors know that early smoking may lead to other obsessive behaviors, including use of illegal drugs and compulsive food-related problems.

(continued from page 3)

▶ Anorexia nervosa is self-starvation, usually diagnosed when a person's weight drops to 15 percent less than expected according to growth charts.

▶ Bulimia nervosa—binge eating plus purging—is not defined according to a specific weight loss, but by a regular pattern of eating large amounts of food followed by behaviors to eliminate the food, such as vomiting, laxative use, or excessive exercise.

▶ Binge-eating disorder—recurrent episodes of bingeing, or compulsive overeating, followed by periods of guilt and disgust—occurs without the purging behavior.

Doctors recognize other disorders, as well, including exercise that becomes an obsession and is practiced for many hours a day, and a collection of disordered eating patterns labeled "eating disorders not otherwise specified," or *EDNOS*.

Later chapters in this book will provide more details about all of these conditions, as well as about the causes, which are complex. They come from a combination of physical, mental, emotional, and social sources that are difficult even for professionals to untangle. But what is clear today is that these forms of self-destruction are not simply bad habits or difficult behavior that can be controlled. They are medical conditions that require professional attention.

They can be hard to live with, and can be hard to understand. A teen with an eating disorder has a big gap between how she really looks and the way she sees herself. Then, once she is starved to a certain degree, it may become even harder for her to see her body accurately, even though those around her can watch her getting thinner and thinner. It can be really frustrating, but it's important to know that the person isn't doing this on purpose. Eating disorders are not due to stubbornness or willfulness. Rather, they are real, treatable medical illnesses in which unhealthy patterns of eating take on a life of their own.

In that way these physical problems can be seen as mental problems as well. Eating disorders often come along with other psychiatric disorders such as depression, substance abuse, and *anxiety disorders.* If you look closely at someone whose eating seems disordered, you're likely to see someone who may be emotionally stressed out as a result of troubling events in their past or present. Also, as we'll explain in more detail in the next chapters, eating disorders are considered psychiatric illnesses in their own right. People with eating disorders, for example, experience obsessive thoughts that compel them to practice irrational behavior. Researchers are also finding evidence that disorders in brain functions are connected with these conditions.

With such specific descriptions and so much information on eating disorders, one might think them simple to diagnose. Unfortunately, *denial* makes it a lot less simple. Denial is a kind of mental blindness that makes people not want to see something that is really there. A teen who feels the need to be thin may not be able to see how skinny she's getting. Her parents may be so frightened of her condition that they unconsciously force themselves not to see it.

WHAT EATING DISORDERS AREN'T

It's not just denial that causes confusion about eating disorders. As we've seen, they aren't always what they seem. Are you confused? You may be worried that you are headed for an eating disorder, but you may be confused about the actual facts. One important fact is that, according to a survey by the National Eating Disorders Association, 96 percent of Americans believe that eating disorders are serious illnesses. This is good news, because it means support for research and treatment. But there is still confusion, because not all unusual eating patterns are actually disorders.

Not only are there various types of eating disorders, but the problem also has different names: eating illness, food *compulsions,* food *addiction,* obsessive eating. Plus, a more general term for a problem that affects even more young people: perhaps 5 percent—nearly 1.5 million—experience disordered eating, or some form of unhealthy obsession with food and body image that stops short of those more serious diagnoses.

It can also be tricky to differentiate among true eating disorders and less dangerous developmental patterns. For instance, the following can be signs of an eating disorder or simply typical patterns of adolescent development:

> ▸ Mood swings: Hormonal changes affecting teens, *or* psychiatric conditions occurring with eating disorders
> ▸ Concern with appearance: Teens newly aware of looking just right, *or* people with eating disorders obsessed with their bodies
> ▸ Menstrual problems: Teen girls taking a while to establish regular periods, *or* eating and exercise interfering with periods
> ▸ Withdrawal from family: Adolescents needing to separate as part of growth, *or* secrecy and isolation that characterizes eating disorders

If you're wondering whether you have an eating disorder, you need to check it out. One way of thinking about it is to see if your habits are in some kind of balance. For instance, a woman was worried about her daughter, who had just started a very stressful program at college and had started running five miles every night "to combat stress," she said. She had also started a "healthy eating" program and had lost almost 20 pounds, though she had not been overweight. When she began to have menstrual problems, her mother consulted a professional. The girl denied any eating issues, and her mother says that she does eat a variety of food.

To clarify if the daughter has an eating disorder, or has simply lost weight due to stress or some other temporary condition, the doctor asks: Is she eating a full variety of food without anxiety? Can she stop losing weight and gain some back by adding higher-calorie foods? Can she be flexible enough to change her eating and exercise patterns, and eat more and exercise less without showing anxiety, and plan other ways to reduce stress?

The doctor tells this mother that if people are eating a full range of foods, without anxiety, and are flexible in setting out more adaptive patterns for managing challenges in their lives, they probably don't have an eating disorder. However, if they have problems with these changes, they may have slipped into an eating disorder. It's important to note that it was not the girl, but her mother, who sought help. One clue to an eating disorder is the inability to see it for one's self, so that was a cause for concern.

Here are some other ways to evaluate a true eating disorder:

> *Feeling fit versus fearing fat.* Being fit is fine; going over the line into rigid exercise may be dangerous.
> *Growth spurt.* Teens and preteens eat differently from when they were younger: They may eat a lot as they get ready to grow.
> *Adolescent rebellion.* The more you're told, "It's good for you," the more likely you are to not do it, right? The teen years are a time to rebel against rules, even when the rules are helpful.
> *Picky eating.* If you've always been a picky eater, you probably still are.

Do these patterns sound familiar to you? You probably know at least a couple of kids who make a big deal out of some kind of dieting—and even more who are really focused on "looking good." This kind of self-focus is common among young teens, who are going through a stage where they're really trying to get to know themselves. Unfortunately, it comes at a time when a young person's body is itself growing through uncomfortable and not always attractive stages—so it's natural that kids seek out some way to look better. The problems arise when, feeling that you can't control your growth patterns or all the new stuff in your life, you focus on something you can control, like your food intake. You'll have opportunities throughout this book to evaluate your own relationship to food. Whether your concern is for yourself or for a friend or family member, eating disorders *do* matter to you.

WHY THEY MATTER TO YOU, NOW

Almost all eating disorders start during adolescence, and they may last as long 15 or 20 years, for those who survive, so the more you know about them now, the better the chance for gaining a deeper understanding.

This book can give you the chance to get information you need to make healthy choices about your body and to make sense of behavior you may see in your friends or family. You'll find facts that will guide you to smart decisions, beginning with what causes disordered eating and exercise.

The causes of eating disorders are complex, involving a combination of physiological, psychological, genetic, social, and family factors. As we'll detail in chapter 3, the causes are to a great extent still under study, but the dangers are real.

➤ Children and teens diagnosed with anorexia have a 5–7 percent chance of dying within 10 years, and those with bulimia have a risk of dying within five years, from their disease or from suicide.

➤ For those who survive, eating disorders can create a wide range of chronic physical health complications, including serious heart conditions and kidney failure.

➤ Eating disorders often occur with other dangerous health patterns—and they are usually a symptom of deeper psychiatric problems that need to be addressed.

Eating disorders are not just fads—they kill. You'll find details in chapter 5 of how eating disorders can be fatal, but death can be hard for a young person to believe in. Dying may seem like such a far-off event that it may be tough to connect it with what seems like a simple diet, when in fact eating disorders can cause a lot of complicated problems that have a more immediate impact. These can include serious heart conditions and kidney failure; disruption in menstrual cycle; irritability; lack of ability to concentrate; blurred vision; kidney

(continues on page 12)

True or False?

1. John never used to be fat, but at 12, he's pudgy. He has an eating disorder. **T/F**

2. Bulimia is a mental disorder. **T/F**

3. Teens with anorexia often boast to family of how much weight they have lost. **T/F**

4. Vomiting when you've overeaten is a safe way to keep from gaining weight. **T/F**

5. Someone can cure an eating disorder just by eating more. **T/F**

6. Eating problems are the family's fault. **T/F**

7. "Pictures don't lie. See how ugly I look?" **T/F**

8. You have to be anorexic to be a dancer. **T/F**

9. Most teens with eating disorders "grow out of them." **T/F**

10. Eating disorders can't be cured. **T/F**

Answers:

1. False. Probably not! Young teens and preteens often go through a normal "pudgy" phase just before the growth spurt that turns them into taller teens. But anyone concerned about a changing size or shape should check with a doctor.

2. True. Bulimia and all other eating disorders are considered psychological disorders, not just physical problems or bad habits.

3. False. Secrecy is a prime characteristic of the behaviors surrounding eating disorders. People with eating disorders usually go to great lengths to conceal them, in part because they don't want to be stopped. They may communicate with others who also have eating disorders, because a sense of mastery over their bodies is part of the motivation.

4. False. Vomiting is the body's way of ridding itself of hazards in emergencies. Throwing up unnecessarily is harmful to many

organs, and also prevents the body from taking in important nutrients.

5. False. Someone with anorexia really can't "eat more" and actively resists being encouraged to eat more. People with bulimia may *purge* more if forced to eat more. Effective treatment involves a careful combination of processes to address the psychological and emotional issues behind the disorder while encouraging a more balanced intake of foods.

6. False. It was once thought that mothers' behavior "caused" eating disorders, but today causes are not viewed so simply. There may be some genetic connections, and family food patterns may often be an influence in children's eating. Teens' food-related behavior may be an act of independence from their families, but there's no one cause to blame.

7. False. In magazines, photos are altered to make the bodies look perfect. Clothes, lighting, and special effects make models look thin. And in the eyes of someone with an eating disorder, pictures definitely lie: They look at photos—or in mirrors—and perceive bodies that are very different from what they look like in reality. Part of treatment is to adjust image to reality.

8. False. Dancing, as well as sports like gymnastics, place a high value on slender bodies, just as other sports seem to demand big muscles. Sometimes more emphasis is placed on body shape than on skills, but today coaches are urged to beware of overstressing body shape. Eating disorders can sap energy and limit performance.

9. False. Some young adults may pass through eating issues like a phase, but eating disorders can be long-term, and early treatment is important because of the damage they can cause, especially to developing bodies.

10. False. If treated with appropriate physical and psychological care, a person with an eating disorder has a 70 percent chance of a full recovery, and the more promptly treatment is begun, the more successful the result.

(continued from page 9)
and/or urinary tract infections; sore throat; dental problems; stomach cramping, blood in stools or vomit, diarrhea, constipation, and/or incontinence; insomnia; fatigue; anxiety; or depression.

Understanding eating disorders is important because, as a teen, you are ready to make serious decisions on your own. To make good decisions, you need to judge the value of the source of the information you receive. As we've already seen, media messages strongly influence young people's decisions, so you'll read here about how to judge the messages the media send you.

It's not easy to live with an eating disorder, whether in yourself or your family or friends. The good news is that all of these dangerous disorders can be treated, but treatment may be long-term and ongoing. Managing eating disorders—living with them and living within the cultural environment that promotes disordered eating—is a challenge: one which this book will help you meet.

Experts note that while it is too simple to say that eating disorders are *caused* by dieting, the fact is, they usually begin with a diet. If you are like most people your age, you are living under a lot of natural pressures—from within your own body, from peers, from family, and from society at large—especially in an age when the Internet and other media pound ideas and images at you 24 hours a day, seven days a week. Yet a process such as dieting, begun to get control of your body, can end up controlling you instead.

Awareness of the actual facts can make a life-or-death difference to you and your friends and family. Awareness is the first step toward making any change, and when we're dealing with eating disorders, forces like denial—a kind of blindness—and secrecy can work against facing facts. This book provides an opportunity to learn in private the facts about eating disorders. To help you better understand the information here, and to find more information and practical help, at the back of the book is a glossary of terms and extra sections including further reading suggestions and contact information for organizations and support groups.

One big piece of good news that you will discover as you go through this book: Whether you are concerned about managing your own eating disorder, or about living with one in someone you care about, you are not alone! In the listings at the back of the book, you'll find plenty of organizations, informal groups, and support networks to guide you and your family and friends.

Eating disorders can be frightening. Facts go a long way to remove fear, so read on to find detailed facts on eating disorders, their causes, and treatments.

WHAT YOU NEED TO KNOW

➤ Eating disorders are especially important for teens to understand, since most of these disorders begin in adolescence.

➤ Eating disorders are the result of complicated physical, mental, and social interactions.

➤ Eating disorders usually begin with a diet, but reach a point where the body may not be able to stop without treatment.

➤ Eating disorders can be treated.

2

A Closer Look at Eating Disorders

***Anorexia* comes from the Greek for "without hunger."** *Bulimia* literally means "ox-like hunger." Those definitions are remnants of a time when the disorders were misunderstood. Early researchers were told by subjects that the reason they didn't eat was that they "weren't hungry," while people with bulimia seemed to eat a lot ("like an ox"), but were throwing up nearly everything they ate. In reality, people with anorexia nervosa do possess an appetite, while people with bulimia do not possess unusual hunger. The word *nervosa* indicates what earlier researchers were beginning to realize: that there was a psychological aspect to the disorders. It was recognized that while they seem to be about "eating or not eating food," such food-related behavior is connected to some deeper emotional and psychological matters. Diagnosis is a lot more accurate today, and despite the pattern of secrecy, the good news is that most people and many researchers are so familiar with these painful illnesses that people do know their names and something about them. Until fairly recently this kind of attention was rare, so people suffered without help, but this does not mean that eating disorders are new to humankind.

It's not just modern-day celebrities who make news by being too thin. The hieroglyphics of ancient Egypt and early manuscripts from ancient Persia, as well as writings from the earliest Chinese dynasties, describe activities related to what we call anorexia and bulimia. Those couches that we see in scenes from ancient Roman banquets were used so that the parties could more easily overeat—and then

14

go to special rooms called vomitoria where they could throw up and make more room for feasting.

Other stories, from Africa, tell of mothers who refused food during famines to save the little bit of food for their children. This became such an admired habit that some of them continued to refuse food.

Historians say that in Europe, the first formal description of anorexia nervosa in medical literature was made in London in 1689 by a doctor who first described an anorexic patient as "a skeleton clad only with skin." The first medical articles about anorexia were not written until 1874, and it was not until the 1930s that researchers began to believe that the causes of self-starvation included psychological problems. Today it is seen as a combination of emotional distress with physiological imbalance, caused in part by social factors.

JUST THE FACTS

All eating disorders are similar in that they are physical, psychological, and social disturbances, though the specific patterns differ for each type. For example, the physical side of anorexia involves self-starvation, while a physical aspect of bulimia results in damage to teeth and stomach from purging. When physicians examine someone with an eating disorder, they often find malnutrition, *dehydration*, ruptured stomach or esophagus, and serious heart, kidney, and liver damage.

Psychologically, most sufferers employ denial—they refuse to believe or to admit the facts that a doctor can show them. Other psychological symptoms that professionals observe in those with eating disorders include depression, guilt and shame, mood swings, perfectionism, and "all or nothing" thinking.

Socially, eating disorders involve increasing isolation from others. Some of this is by choice—to protect the disorder's ritualistic patterns. But also, the sufferers' feelings and obsessions damage family and social relationships.

You may observe some of these symptoms and behaviors in people you care about. You may feel hurt when shut out of someone's life, so it's especially important to understand that people with eating disorders *are* suffering, and that their withdrawal isn't meant to be personal. So let's take a closer look.

ANOREXIA

Do you know anyone who sees him or herself as overweight even though this person is dangerously thin? Anorexia affects mostly girls, but boys can have it as well. They seem always to be weighing themselves, and for them, eating and not eating becomes an obsession. Do you notice people with really unusual eating habits—like avoiding food and meals, picking out a few foods and eating only a few foods, in small quantities, or carefully weighing and dividing portions? You may also see them involved in intensive exercise, and they may also try to control weight by vomiting or using *laxatives,* enemas, and *diuretics.* Specialists recognize the following two types of anorexia nervosa:

- Restricting type: Keeping weight low by simply not eating
- Binge-eating/Purging type: Adding purging to dieting—like those with bulimia, they induce vomiting or keep their bodies "empty" by using laxatives, diuretics, or enemas

Symptoms are both physical and emotional in nature. Anorexia is defined as "Refusal to maintain or achieve a body weight of 85 percent of the expected weight for the person's age and height." This means that if a normal weight would be 120, an unhealthy weight would be maintained at 102 or less. (Adults meet this condition through losing weight, but adolescents who do not gain weight normally as they grow can become underweight without weight loss). Note that this is "refusal"—not inability. Some young adults naturally become skinny as they grow quickly; others may try to gain weight but can't. People with anorexia actively won't add pounds, and often their weight gets progressively lower. One sign of unhealthily low weight or excessive exercise in women is *amenorrhea*—the absence of at least three consecutive menstrual cycles (or in young teens, an unusual delay in the start of menstruation).

Those with this disorder suffer an intense fear of gaining weight or becoming fat, even if considered underweight. They also commonly experience distortion of body image, excess focus on body shape, or denial of low-weight problem; low self-esteem; and fear of losing control in many areas of daily living.

BULIMIA

You may have a harder time recognizing someone with bulimia than with anorexia, because bulimia doesn't usually cause a dramatic weight loss. You may think of bulimia as involving vomiting, but as we noted, sometimes anorexia does, too. Since binge eating is always present in bulimia, the purging, by vomiting or other means, is an attempt to counter the overeating and to maintain weight. Someone with bulimia wants to maintain or lose weight, but goes to great lengths to do that. You may notice someone who "disappears" after meals—or who seems to make a lot of visits to the bathroom. But you may also know someone who spends a lot more time at the gym, or maybe he begins to go on fasts. Exercise and occasional fasting may be healthy, but they can serve as healthy fronts for people with an obsession to overeat and not gain weight. If you know someone who fasts for religious reasons or goes overboard at the gym briefly, that's probably not unusual: Specialists note that to qualify as a disorder, the weight-fighting activities must be practiced at least twice a week for at least three months.

In sum, there are the following two types of bulimia, and neither type insists on being underweight:

▶ Purging type: Vomiting or the abuse of laxatives, diuretics, or enemas to compensate for compulsive eating
▶ Non-purging type: Compensating only by exercise or fasting

Physical signs of bulimia include the eating of a larger amount of food in a shorter amount of time than do most people, followed by behavior to compensate for binges: vomiting, abuse of laxatives/ diuretics, fasting, and excessive exercise. People with bulimia maintain near-normal weight because they compensate for their overeating with overexercise or purging. But other physical symptoms include frequent, often serious, problems with teeth and the digestive system because of the disruptions caused by purging activities. Emotionally, people with bulimia feel a compulsion to overeat, a panicky sense that one cannot stop or control intake. They suffer a distortion of their body image, caused by an excess critical focus on their body shape, which they always think is "too big" or "too ugly." They tend to fear losing control in many areas of daily living, and when they can't remain in control they feel fear and shame, which they turn to the eating disorder to ease. Their behavior may actually increase their sense of shame and depression, since most realize their disorder is unusual and dangerous. Overall, like most people with eating disorders, they may live with a low sense of self-esteem, which may lead to the disorder and may in turn increase their feelings of low self-esteem.

It is also important to know that eating disorders can occur along a spectrum. Some teenagers may start with anorexia and have their disorder evolve or change to bulimia and have episodes of both disorders.

BINGE-EATING DISORDER

Although *binge-eating disorder* (BED) is not yet an official diagnosis according to the American Psychiatric Association, you may know someone who goes on compulsive food binges. This isn't like chowing down for holidays, or gorging on popcorn while watching a scary movie. You can almost sense the powerful urge that's connected with this kind of overeating. Researchers recognize it, too, and some say it's almost twice as common as anorexia or bulimia. Someone who is a binge eater is likely to be overweight and unhappy about it. BED is defined as recurrent episodes of binge eating—eating an excessive amount of food in a short period of time, while feeling a sense of lack of control.

Physical symptoms of BED include eating though not feeling hungry and continuing until feeling uncomfortably full. The binge eating occurs at least two days a week for six months and consists of high-fat, high-calorie foods like chips and ice cream. Weight gain is evident and the binge eating is not associated with purging, fasting, or excessive exercise.

Emotionally, those with BED may be using binges as a way to hide from their emotions, to fill a void they feel inside, or to cope with daily stresses and problems in their lives. The individual may feel disgusted with himself, depressed, or very guilty after overeating. There is clear distress about the binge-eating behavior.

Many with the disorder are overweight for their age and height. Feelings of self-disgust and shame associated with this illness can lead to bingeing again, creating a cycle of binge eating.

COMPULSIVE OVEREATING

Compulsive overeating is what some would call an "eating addiction"— eating more food than is needed, in situations where it makes no sense. Of all the eating disorders, it's one that affects men and boys almost as much as women and girls. It's different from binge eating in that it occurs on a more regular basis. It's "emotional eating" in that people may use food and eating as a way to hide from their emotions, to fill an inner void or to cope with stress.

Symptoms displayed by compulsive overeaters include diseases associated with obesity, because they tend to be overweight. It is the emotional aspects of overeating that can be particularly strong. For instance, the excess weight may protect a person from dealing with potentially painful relationships. Often, though, the very feelings that the eating is meant to soothe come back because of the eating. In a negative cycle for compulsive overeaters; the guilt, shame, and low self-esteem caused by their overweight may trigger them to eat more.

EATING DISORDER NOT OTHERWISE SPECIFIED

Eating Disorder Not Otherwise Specified (EDNOS) refers to any kind of eating pattern that is "disordered" or irrational, but which doesn't fit specific guidelines for other types. For instance:

➤ Someone who meets all the criteria for anorexia nervosa but continues to have normal menstrual cycles, or who can maintain weight in the "normal" range
➤ A person who meets all the criteria for bulimia nervosa, but who has been doing it for less than three months or less often than twice weekly
➤ There is no bingeing but there is purging, laxative use, excessive exercise, or other behaviors after eating small amounts of food
➤ Continued chewing and spitting out large amounts of food without swallowing
➤ Someone who binges and purges, but not in reaction to her perception of body shape

Binge-eating disorder is officially an EDNOS.

The emotional and physical symptoms of EDNOS conditions are similar to those of the more "standard" eating disorders, with some variations. One is "night eating syndrome," where a person does most of his or her eating at the evening meal and later, into the night, when the desire to eat often interrupts sleep.

With all those definitions and information, is there an easy way to understand eating disorders? If your focus is on eating or not eating, and it persists when it makes no logical sense—and causes more problems than it solves—you may have a problem.

DISORDERED EATING

All of the above eating disorders fall under the broad category of disordered eating. In a culture where the media urge us to cook and eat rich foods and offer us "sure thing" diets; where we worry about obese children but warn against early dieting—we could say that our society's view of food and weight is "disordered." This may be so common that it's hard to recognize it in an individual. But disordered eating can get in the way of daily life when a person's attitudes about food, weight, and body size lead to very rigid eating and exercise habits that make life painful. Disordered eating may begin as a way to lose a few pounds or get in shape, but these behaviors can get out of control, become obsessions, and may even turn into an eating disorder. When you see someone who seems to pay too much attention to weighing, calorie-counting, or exercise, he or she may be dealing with disordered eating—and missing out on some of the more satisfying parts of life.

Do any of those descriptions sound familiar? Eating-disorder specialists point out that focusing on a specific diagnosis can be misleading—it's too easy to think, "Well, I don't have that one symptom . . . so I must not have a disorder."

A simpler rule of thumb to evaluate a person with food-focused disorders is just to ask, "Are you thinking about weight, food, and *calories,* too much? Are you engaging in unhealthy behaviors to control your weight?"

SOME MORE CLUES

Most people with eating disorders try to hide their problems. But some problems connected with eating disorders aren't easy to keep secret. Anxiety and depression are often associated with eating disorders. Personality disorders like OCD (obsessive-compulsive disorder) are also often found among those with eating disorders.

When unusual eating behavior is combined with some disturbing behaviors that don't seem connected with food, there can be added cause for concern. Those with eating disorders often engage in cutting, burning, or other forms of self-harm, using some form of sharp edge to draw blood, or burning skin or hair—or even being drawn to abusive relationships. This produces a feeling of relief for some. Others, who may be "emotionally numb," say that any feeling is welcome.

In *body dysmorphic disorder,* there is overfocus on some body part or body-shape seen as defective. This has much in common with eating disorders, but it doesn't involve food issues. It can feel overwhelming, and a person may continually look in mirrors and spend so much energy obsessing that he or she can't function.

Eating disorders have some important factors in common, including the factors that put a person at risk for developing them. Professionals who treat eating disorders have come up with this list of risks that could increase the chance of developing eating disorders:

➤ Intense weight concerns before age 14
➤ High level of perceived stress
➤ Behavior problems before age 14

- History of dieting
- Mother diets and is concerned about appearance
- Siblings diet and are concerned about appearance
- Peers diet and are concerned about appearance
- Negative self-evaluation
- Perfectionism
- No friends of opposite sex
- Parental control
- Intense rivalry with one or more siblings
- Competitive with siblings' shape and/or appearance
- Shy and/or anxious
- Distressed by parental arguments
- Distressed by life events occurring in the year before the illness develops
- Critical comments from family members about weight, shape, and eating
- Teasing about weight, shape, and appearance

GETTING PERSONAL

As you can tell from all that information, many risk factors are known for eating disorders. Important as they are, it's even more important to look at how they affect individual people. Here are some ways of taking a closer, more personal look at whether an eating disorder is affecting someone's life.

Someone who may have an eating disorder may be familiar with these following situations:

- Avoids eating when hungry
- Cuts food into small pieces
- Feels guilty after eating
- Feels terrified about being overweight
- Has gone on eating binges without being able to stop
- Is overly concerned about the calorie content of foods
- Is preoccupied with a desire to be thinner
- Uses laxatives or water pills to keep weight down
- Thinks he or she is not good enough or is worthless; judged in a negative way
- Takes longer than others to eat meals
- Seeks approval from people and has a hard time saying no
- Is preoccupied with the thought of having fat on his or her body

> ‣ Is considered the "strong one" to whom everyone goes with problems
> ‣ Is a perfectionist or overachiever and never feels "good enough"
> ‣ Eats diet foods
> ‣ Tries to avoid foods he or she believes contain sugar
> ‣ Begins to think of some foods as "bad"
> ‣ Is preoccupied with food
> ‣ Particularly avoids food with a high carbohydrate or fat content
> ‣ Thinks about burning up calories while exercising
> ‣ Vomits after eating
> ‣ Comes from a turbulent or confusing family background
> ‣ Feels proud and strong at being able to deprive self of food
> ‣ Has thoughts and plans centered on food or exercise
> ‣ Moves from controlling overweight to maintaining underweight
> ‣ Started exercising one hour a day and now does three or four
> ‣ Thinks life would be better or people would like them more if they were thinner

Some of the items on this list may surprise you, but they all are characteristic of different aspects of eating disorders. While you were reading the list of characteristics, did any of the descriptions seem to apply to your own life or behavior? If so, you might want to take them to a doctor for help in evaluating whether you might be headed for an eating disorder.

LOOKING FOR ADVICE

As you've probably figured out by now, eating disorders are not a matter of choice, willpower, or vanity. They are true diseases, and once they take hold, they can be dangerous. So it's worth checking with a professional. Your family doctor may be helpful, but many people find they're better off with specialists. Ask questions to help you form an opinion of the doctor's qualifications. If the physician doesn't seem like a good fit, keep looking, or ask for names of other doctors who would be qualified.

Many types of specialists deal with eating disorders, including dietitians, nutritionists, and therapists. If you're just beginning to explore eating-related issues, you may want simply to talk with a friend who is in treatment for a disorder, to find out what it's like. Or you might feel more comfortable getting information off the Internet. You need to be especially careful in selecting safe and worthwhile Web sources. Here are some good ones, where you can find reliable information as well as guides to professional help:

> The National Eating Disorders Association (http://www.national eatingdisorders.org) is a source for facts and support, and the entries for treatment providers are very descriptive, including treatment methods, payment options, credentials, and subspecialties. Helpful support-group entries are also included.
> Something Fishy Treatment Finder (http://www.something-fishy.org/treatmentfinder) is a comprehensive resource, with thousands of entries of various kinds. It includes categories broken down by treatment type, location, and approach.
> About.com: Eating Disorders (http://eatingdisorders.about.com) is another excellent online resource for facts and further info.

Some people are reluctant to take a closer look at their own signs of eating disorders. Sometimes this can be due to fear or shame. Eating disorders needn't be cause for shame. Recovering from them is not just a matter of "eating properly" or "getting yourself together." These are conditions that require extra help and in-depth understanding.

Many of us eat too much sometimes. Many of us also may go on diets or on exercise campaigns that may or may not succeed. Those are not eating disorders. For some, those experiences can trigger a compulsive pattern that develops into a destructive, unmanageable pattern. They may not be dangerous yet, but eating disorders tend to be progressive, so early signs of eating disorders indicate a need for professional help in keeping them from getting worse.

WHAT YOU NEED TO KNOW

> Eating disorders have been around for many centuries.
> Eating disorders are physical, mental, emotional, and social conditions.
> Eating disorders take many different forms.
> Eating disorders require professional help for treatment.

3

Causes of Eating Disorders

One teenaged girl hides in the bathroom and eats till she "feels sick." Another focuses only on not eating, cutting her food into tiny bits and spitting out most of it. A tenth-grade boy lets his grades drop while he spends hours at the gym. A new college freshman spends most of her orientation week finding where all the bathrooms are, so she can throw up whenever she needs to get rid of food.

When we take a close look at the facts of eating disorders and how people who have them act in self-destructive ways, we can see how powerful those diseases are. We also get a clue as to how complicated the causes of these powerful diseases must be.

It should be simple, you might think: You feel hungry, you eat, you process food. But it seems that the whole physiology and psychology of food and eating are extremely complex, involving signals between the brain and the other organs, set off by sets of external and internal triggers. It actually doesn't take much—a misfiring of some internal or environmental message—to upset the natural balance of this system. Think about times when you were nervous, and you may have eaten too much. Or remember when you were very worried or sad and didn't feel like eating at all. That gives you an idea of the connections between emotions, food, and behavior.

Exactly how eating gets disordered is not yet fully known. Science started seriously researching these disorders only a short time ago, but research is beginning to show details of the physical connections that are involved in eating disorders. But it is clear that disordered eating may be seen as a physical, mental, and social disease: physical, including brain chemistry; psychological, including developmental issues; and social, including family and the media.

PHYSICAL CAUSES

*A **brain disease?*** In recent years, scientists have been able to achieve so much in brain research that they have a better idea than ever before of the physical role that the brain plays in eating disorders, as well as in addictions and other conditions that people once considered simply the result of weak wills. The results of this research have been so dramatic that in 2006 the head of the National Institute of Mental Health (NIMH) declared, "Anorexia is a brain disease." What he means is this: The brain's chemical and electrical systems influence things in our bodies. The brain sends nerve messages that stimulate the body chemicals called neurotransmitters—and in eating disorders, these systems aren't functioning correctly.

Scientists have learned that both appetite and energy levels are regulated by a complex network of nerve cells and chemical messengers called neuropeptides. They have focused recently on the neuroendocrine system—a combination of the central nervous system and the network of body chemicals called hormones. This linkage of electrical impulses and chemical connectors creates a carefully balanced mechanism that regulates such critical body conditions as sexual function, physical growth and development, appetite and digestion, sleep, heart and kidney function, emotions, thinking, and memory. These regulatory mechanisms are (1) fueled by the food the body takes in and breaks down to simple chemicals, and (2) influence the balancing of hunger and activity. When researchers studied these chemical balances, they discovered the following:

> ▸ Connections exist between stress-related hormones and eating disorders.
> ▸ Excess levels of depression-related hormones are present in some people with anorexia.
> ▸ Brain-chemistry similarities exist between people with eating disorders and those with obsessive-compulsive disorder (OCD). Many patients with bulimia have severe OCD, and many with OCD have eating disorders.

➤ A brain hormone that makes us feel full enough to stop eating is too low in some people with bulimia.

➤ Dopamine, involved with feelings of pleasure, is disordered in people with anorexia, which may be why they don't experience a sense of pleasure from food and other comforts.

So there are many connections between eating activity and brain functions. Some studies show that abnormalities in brain proteins may make a person more vulnerable to eating disorders. What is not yet known is whether chemical imbalances cause eating disorders or whether the abnormal eating causes the imbalances. Still, the more scientists know about the connections between disordered eating and brain chemicals, the better they can understand the disorders.

Another important observation from brain researchers is that the parts of the brain most involved with eating disorders are also those involved with making judgments and decisions. As a teen, that part of your brain is still developing—so when eating disorders are added to the mix, it can impact how you make decisions about life.

Biological causes. Age is included in the risk factors for eating disorders, in part because the teen years are when most of these disorders start. It's also the age when important hormones are shifting.

Gender appears to be another factor in eating disorders. Females appear more likely to have an eating disorder than males. Only an estimated 5–15 percent of people with anorexia or bulimia and an estimated 35 percent of those with binge-eating disorder are male. This may have to do with hormones or body-image issues. Some psychologists would look to a girl's relationship with her mother. Or it could be due to a combination of all these factors.

Can you inherit eating disorders? Scientists can't be sure, but they see genetics affecting over half of people with anorexia. There is some evidence that there may be a genetic vulnerability to some personality types or temperaments, such as obsessive-compulsive disorder or high levels of anxiety, that make one more prone to eating disorders. A girl with a mother or sister who has had anorexia nervosa is 12 times more likely to develop the disorder than others with no family history; those with a mother or sister with bulimia are four times more likely to develop it themselves.

It was once thought that eating disorders were mainly a "white woman's disease." Now it is seen to affect African Americans and

Asians as well: Increasing numbers of non-Caucasian women and men develop eating disorders, which is thought perhaps to be due in part to the widening global influence of media-spread images.

FAMILY BACKGROUND

Once, even professionals believed that the family was the primary cause for a child's eating disorder. Different families have different attitudes toward food—some overfeed, some constantly criticize "imperfections." There's probably no one type that is more likely to contribute to disordered eating, but families where there is emotional turbulence or abuse can factor into the development of eating disorders. Likewise, families that are too rigid in their own need for perfection can contribute to a child feeling inadequate, as can families that are too distant to give proper attention to a child. Any of these family factors can play a part in the development of an eating disorder.

There are changes that families can make to relieve the kinds of pressure that can promote eating disorders. One simple way for parents to influence their children's eating habits and to prevent weight problems and eating disorders, according to some research, is to have healthy eating habits themselves. Having frequent family meals together also helps support positive food-related experiences.

Think about it: If your mother keeps wanting you to "clean your plate," you might react by overeating or rebel against it and refuse to eat. If your dad makes disparaging comments about your chubby cheeks, you might want to get rid of them, to please him, or you might want to get chubbier, to make him mad. A boy who's expected to be the "man of the family" might feel he needs to eat a lot to be large enough for that role—or might eat less because he's not ready for the role.

What are the food facts of your family? If you feel that you're making eating decisions in overreaction to family patterns, you might want to take a look at how your emotions may lead to unhealthy eating habits.

PSYCHOLOGICAL FACTORS

Whatever the source of the psychological needs, control and comfort are the two words that probably best sum up the needs that are filled by eating disorders. Trauma—a big upset or long-term turbulence in life—can influence someone to do whatever they can to bring control to life, and food and weight can be easy targets for control.

True or False?

1. People with bulimia feel both pride and shame at the same time.   T/F

2. Someone with anorexia may feel strong as he or she grows physically weak.   T/F

3. Eating causes bulimia.   T/F

4. Starving causes anorexia.   T/F

5. Dieting may trigger an eating disorder.   T/F

6. If I eat only vegetables I'll be okay.   T/F

7. Women on TV wear the same size clothes as real-life women.   T/F

8. Eating is a good way to relieve stress.   T/F

9. Facts you find on the Internet are always accurate.   T/F

Answers:

1. True. People with bulimia take pride in a sense of "mastery," but they may feel ashamed about their bingeing and purging.

2. True. He or she is proud to be strong enough to control his or her body, so the thinner the individual gets, the stronger he or she may feel mentally—but the body will continue to weaken and break down.

Undereating and overeating have been shown to activate calming brain chemicals, which may be why those experiencing emotional pain turn to these eating patterns.

"Mastery" is also an important aspect of eating-disorder psychology. This is the sense that one can reach an achievement that others can't—even if that "achievement" is a too-strict diet.

Personalities. According to psychologists at the National Institute of Mental Health, most people with eating disorders share these

3. False. Overeating is one feature of bulimia, but eating is a natural, healthy function.

4. False. Self-starvation is one feature and result of anorexia. People who are starving can eat when food is available; people with anorexia refuse to gain weight and eat very little.

5. True. In the great majority of cases, an eating disorder begins with a diet, and persistent unhealthy eating can change the brain networks that control eating behavior.

6. False. Limiting intake to one type of food is often a sign of an eating disorder. Being a vegetarian means finding a way to eat a balanced diet without meat; eating only one food out of fear is disordered eating.

7. False. On TV, 85 percent of women wear size four; the average size for real-life women is 12.

8. True and False. Sometimes hunger and body-sugar imbalances can make you feel anxious, which eating nutritious food can resolve. But binge eating or other kinds of disordered eating can lead to increased anxiety.

9. False. Some of the facts you will find on the Internet are true and some are false. Fad Web sites and misinformation can be very dangerous when the topic is eating disorders. In-person professional resources are safer to rely on.

personality characteristics: low self-esteem, perfectionism, feelings of helplessness, and anxiety. They have overly high expectations and have "all-or-nothing" thinking patterns. Can you see how these traits connect to overcontrol of eating? The problem is, disordered eating patterns aren't triggered by these characteristics, but they may make it more difficult to recover.

Emotional causes. Anger and other emotions that are not expressed easily can feed a disorder. In fact, therapists believe that eating disorders are more about trying to relieve uncomfortable feelings and solving life problems than they are about food. The person often is afraid to express these emotions verbally and directly, so he or she does it indirectly through disordered eating patterns. For some, a strong emotion will trigger an eating binge. Others may overeat to mask and numb-out difficult emotions. Non-eaters are able to feel *something,* even if it's physical pain, which may be easier to deal with than their actual emotions.

SOCIAL CAUSES

If it seems that eating disorders are confusing, just think for a moment about the confusing messages we receive about food. Meals are super-sized, physical activity is restricted for personal safety, and people are criticized for obesity. We tell little kids to eat less, but worry if teens aren't eating enough. Babies are "good" if they eat the whole jar, but when they're older they're teased for being chubby.

Studies have shown that overweight people face discrimination in school and at work, but that people in general are growing more and more overweight in the early 21st century.

The pressure to be slim is especially strong among teens, who tend to judge by appearances first. In junior high and high school, the pressure to look good translates into wanting to be the "right" shape and fit into the "right" clothes. This can be tough, when everyone is built differently and teen bodies are changing so fast. Since young people who are vulnerable to eating disorders tend to be lonely and isolated, they may be willing to adapt their appearance to fit in with a group of peers.

Triggers. For those already vulnerable to eating disorders, it may take just a small push to set off the disorder—and pressure to fit in with peers is a lot more than a small push. A trigger can be any kind of event a person doesn't know how to handle—from something as "minor" as being teased to something as major as assault or family death.

A trigger can be something that sets off feelings buried in the past: A coach's criticism may make you feel the way you did when your dad made fun of you; a friend's departure may make you feel the way you did when your childhood pet ran away. Or a trigger can be an event that places new and unexpected demands on you—the loss of a family job, or the departure of an older sibling, or just starting a higher grade at school.

Have you ever been in a situation where you feel inadequate, and look around you at others who seem to be so together? That's a

Pieces of the Puzzle

Here's Andrea's story again. When you read about the causes and results of her eating disorder, see if you can tell how all the "puzzle pieces" fit together.

At **age 12,** Andrea felt that her life would be **perfect** if only she were more slender. Life was pretty **confusing** right now: She sometimes didn't even know who she was, and her family seemed to be always in **turmoil.** Her **parents were fighting** a lot and her brother had just left for the army. Plus, middle school was so much harder than last year, and her **best friends had gone** to other schools. All of a sudden everything seemed to be about her "future": she was **expected** to get good grades, be a good athlete, and always look "nice." Andrea **tried to be perfect,** but she didn't always make it–and that made her miserable. Her one escape was into the fantastic **celebrity world** on Web sites, TV, and her favorite magazines. Her favorite personalities looked so **happy there–and they were so thin!** So Andrea started a diet.

Trouble was, Andrea wasn't really fat–she just **"felt" fat.** She also felt that, with so many aspects of her life out of control, one thing she could **control** was her eating. But once she started the diet, **she couldn't stop.** She never seemed to look thin enough in the **mirror,** no matter how much she **starved** herself.

This is one example of how all the different causes–physical, mental, and social–work together to set the stage for an eating disorder. Age 12 is a prime time for adolescent physical and emotional worries. With a family in turmoil–parents fighting and a brother leaving home–and her best friends going to other schools, a lot is new and confusing, and her life feels out of control. In addition, she is expected to do well in sports and school, and look good. Inner stress can trigger a need for comfort. Andrea wants to be perfect and achieve some kind of control over her life, and the happy and perfect celebrities she sees in magazines and online are all so perfect and thin. Unfortunately, this combination of forces at work has led Andrea to start dieting, subsequently leading to her eating disorder.

perfectly natural feeling for someone in a new situation who feels a need for support. Now extend that feeling, and look around you at all the messages and demands you get from the media that surround us and permeate our lives.

Media as trigger. Many experts feel that the media—TV, the Internet, magazines, blogs—have a major influence on eating disorders. Think about it: Did you ever buy something you saw advertised on TV? Of course you have: Advertising and attractive images are designed to be triggers—triggers to buy, but also triggers to want to look like the attractive people in them.

Whatever the specific causes of eating disorders, they all have to do with disordered perceptions of the body. The National Institute of Mental Health sums it up:

> Eating is controlled by many factors, including appetite, food availability, family, peer, and cultural practices, and attempts at voluntary control. Dieting to a body weight leaner than needed for health is highly promoted by current fashion trends, sales campaigns for special foods, and in some activities and professions.

It would be hard to find anyone in modern America who thought she had a perfect body; who didn't compare herself unfavorably with models or actors. But for the vulnerable, a distorted body image is a key factor in triggering eating disorders.

Advertisers heavily market weight-reduction programs and present skinny young models as the ideal (despite the fine print—"results not typical"). At the same time, advertising floods the public with attractive ads for foods, especially junk food.

Even when fashion is criticized for using too-thin models, clothes are designed and displayed for bodies that few real women could match.

One study reported that teenagers who tried hard to look like celebrities were more likely to be constant dieters.

The media's influence on eating disorders lies in the idealization of thin as perfection. In the sidebar, Andrea believes her celebrity heroes are happy because they are thin. Living in our celebrity-mad culture, it's not surprising if teens especially feel they have to look a certain way to be happy or even healthy.

The media factor is growing as an influence. In the early 21st century, an average American child was seeing more than 30,000 TV commercials each year, as well as more than 21 hours of TV a week, plus dozens of magazines and many movies every year. In those media, happy and successful people are almost always portrayed by actors and models who are young, toned, and thin. Their makeup and hair are always perfect.

More recently, all the forms of wireless media have created networks for information that are not verified facts—and for images that are easily just imaginary!

According to a 2007 survey, even so-called health-oriented magazines can contribute to the problem. Five years after reading magazine articles about dieting, teenage girls were more likely to control weight by fasting, vomiting, smoking cigarettes, or abusing laxatives than girls who never read such articles.

There are even Web sites that promote eating disorders. Everywhere they look, boys and girls as young as six are affected by images of the "ideal" lean male or female. Some might eventually try to match those images by going on a diet.

DIETING IS THE TRIGGER

In all that complex mix of physical, psychological, and social dynamics, the one single factor that most experts agree on as a trigger for developing an eating disorder is going on a diet. A study by the National Association of Anorexia Nervosa and Associated Eating

Skinny Models Make All Young Women Feel Worse

Think you're the only one who envies slim models? A recent study found that looking at picture-perfect and rail-thin models may make young women feel worse about their own bodies, regardless of their size or shape.

Previous studies have shown that images of skinny models negatively affect how overweight women and those with eating disorders view their own body image. But this new study suggests that women feel unhappy about themselves after looking at (airbrushed or computer-enhanced) pictures of models in magazine ads for just three minutes.

Disorders (ANAD) in 2007 found that those who diet moderately are five times more likely to develop eating disorders than those who don't diet. For those who diet "severely," the chances of an eating disorder are 18 times greater.

Dieting may seem innocent and healthy, but going on a diet when you are already at a healthy weight, especially at a young age, combines all three triggering factors: physiological, psychological, and social.

> ▶ *Physiologically,* the food deprivation or nutritional imbalance of a diet can throw the body's systems out of balance, and continued for a while can alter brain chemistry that can set off the chain of events that can lead to an eating disorder. Depriving your body of food can trigger cravings that can lead to binge eating.
> ▶ *Psychologically,* because many severely restrictive diets fail, and in fact can contribute to more weight gain, they can lead to a sense of failure and inadequacy—which can lead to more dieting, and a greater sense of failure, as well as an obsession with working harder at it.
> ▶ *Socially,* dieting is encouraged by the wider world, but it can make personal interaction harder because it may mean refusing invitations to parties or not sharing family meals and snacks. This leads to a sense of isolation, which is a key factor in eating disorders.

WHAT YOU NEED TO KNOW

> ▶ Eating disorders are the result of complex interactions among physiological, psychological, and social factors.
> ▶ Media images are a powerful influence on eating disorders.
> ▶ Most eating disorders begin with a diet.

4

Inside Eating Disorders

"Eating disorders involve serious disturbances in eating behavior, such as extreme and unhealthy reduction of food intake or severe overeating, as well as feelings of distress or extreme concern about body shape or weight." That National Institute of Mental Health summary makes it sound simple, doesn't it? But when we think about words like "serious disturbances," "extreme," and "distress," we can begin to get an idea of what they feel like.

Most of us are familiar with the labels: anorexia, bulimia, bingeing. And we may even know their symptoms—not eating for anorexia, purging for bulimia. . . . But mere labels and scientific descriptions tell only part of the story of Andrea—whose story opened the book. For some people, only a harmful pattern of eating seems to bring relief: someone like 16-year-old Roger, whose obsession with exercise developed into food restriction that landed him in the hospital, or Georgette, 17, who felt compelled to gorge with sweets after every fight with her boyfriend, there is a turbulent emotional side.

People with eating disorders are so good at hiding their feelings and behavior—even at looking tough and in control—that it's sometimes hard to realize the kind of emotional pain they feel. Focusing on what these disorders feel like can be a reminder that they aren't "bad habits" or "fads," but painful conditions that require in-depth understanding and care.

WHAT DOES IT FEEL LIKE?

Chapter 3 talked about how the masking of feelings can be one cause for eating disorders, and how painful feelings can, in turn, trigger disordered-eating episodes. Hearing about those emotions firsthand can help make eating disorders seem real.

The voice of hidden emotions. People with eating disorders may share feelings of inadequacy and fears of not measuring up. They often experience depression, anxiety, guilt, and loneliness. They feel an overwhelming emptiness, a sense of meaninglessness, hopelessness, and despair.

Specialists know that binges and food restrictions both are ways to hide from their emotions, to fill a void they feel inside, and to cope with daily problems.

Here's what they say it *feels* like, living with an eating disorder, in comments made in Internet chat rooms:

> ➤ "When I'm sad, I eat. When I'm lonely, I eat. When I'm bored, I eat. When I'm feeling bad about myself (which is most of the time!), I eat."
>
> ➤ "Emotions control me—make me hide in a safe place of silence. My mind stays distant from what my heart feels. If I say it, it's real, so I say nothing. I can't touch it—if I did I would curl up or crumble. I may seem to have made my heart out of stone, but it's really just chalk, and I'm afraid to face the possibility that I could easily turn to dust."
>
> ➤ "It's not about the weight—it's about the inability to deal with feelings and emotions. About using a bowl of pasta or a pound of M&M's as a narcotic to stem the pain. That's what compulsive overeating is. I cry because it makes me overweight."
>
> ➤ "I'd eat in secret, gorging myself with more food than necessary, way beyond the point of feeling full. Guilt, anxiety, and fear would always ensue. Feelings of rage, hatred, and loathing would follow; or severe depression with suicidal tendencies. You know, it's ironic: I understand my disease enough to know that it all stems from issues of control (feeling out of control and abusing food to regain it). But I am so out of control when I abuse food that it just becomes a vicious circle day after day after day."

What anorexia feels like. Most individuals with anorexia strongly deny it, despite medical tests that have revealed telltale symptoms, and even when they must be hospitalized to prevent permanent damage or even death from starvation. A person with anorexia may become hyperactive, feel dizzy, and feel a "buzz" at all times. He or she may feel depressed, irritable, withdrawn, and be prone to compulsive rituals about food.

One teen explains, "Four years ago, I turned to starvation and purging to fill a huge void in myself. I was in the seventh grade, and I remember how terribly insecure and unhappy I was. I hated the curves that were forming on my body and perceived myself as grossly overweight. In retrospect, I was at a completely healthy weight for my height. I was focusing on my weight and controlling my food intake in order to avoid the unhappiness and insecurity I was really feeling."

She was lucky in that her anorexia didn't last too long—and she can also talk about it. More typical is the young woman who started dieting around the age of 11 after being teased for being pudgy. She had blamed herself for her father's leaving home and was still struggling to "fix it." This began a long series of struggles with dieting, bingeing and purging, and disordered eating. As a teenager she was hospitalized a few times for both anorexia and bulimia and left home at seventeen. She continued to struggle, and would get into balance, only to relapse and fall into a sense of hopelessness from having been in many hospitals, seeing many different therapists and psychiatrists and other doctors, and never attaining health other than to keep her weight loss under control—while still maintaining her food rituals.

What bulimia feels like. In one key aspect, bulimia "feels" different from anorexia to its sufferers. People who have bulimia may be aware that something is seriously wrong rather than be in denial about it, as is so common in anorexia. The self-loathing that characterizes the disorder is given more opportunities to express itself since bulimics report "feeling disgusted" by their perceived overeating, and then again every time they binge. A girl with bulimia is willing to establish complicated life-patterns to allow for her binge-purge behavior. She knows what's going on, but the patterns seem to intensify, rather than lessen, her feelings of isolation and self-hatred.

One young woman with bulimia tells the story of being under stress and rushing to a convenience store where she bought a box of doughnuts. Before even going home, she went behind the store next to a trash bin and frantically stuffed the doughnuts down her throat whole, alone, in the dark. As soon as she got home, she made herself vomit. It helps us to understand how intense are the feelings behind the behavior—and that it is not about food, but about using the behavior itself to escape from her feelings. She describes herself as being in an "altered state" during the process: For people with this eating disorder, bingeing and purging can distract them from their troubles for a time. But the relief that's felt is soon replaced by feelings of guilt and shame, which lead to a need to repeat the cycle.

When you compare the binge-purge experience to the experience of those who cut themselves, you may be able to see how they're connected. People who hurt themselves on purpose explain that it's to release the pain, to escape it, to distract themselves from stress and emotional discomfort. They cut their flesh or burn it. They bang their heads or swallow foreign objects. Some report that while they are engaged in

The Top 10 Ways to Tell when Dieting Becomes a Disorder

It's not "just a diet" when it

- ➤ goes on past the lowest recommended weight
- ➤ involves vomiting
- ➤ involves rituals
- ➤ requires secrecy
- ➤ demands hours of daily exercise
- ➤ means eating only a couple of foods, and in specific sizes and shapes
- ➤ is driven by fear
- ➤ is the main focus of your day
- ➤ features self-loathing when you "slip" a bit
- ➤ feels like it's never enough

Those characteristics may be signs of eating disorders and signs of self-hatred, rather than a good diet that is meant to be good for your health.

self-harm, they may experience peace, tranquility, and calm—a sense of being grounded after feeling tossed about by chaos and misery—at least for a while, until stress and tension mount again.

It may be hard for those who don't share this kind of behavior to understand it. And even when they find others who share their experience, there's still a strong need to keep it secret. The secrecy is part of the process and it's also part of the pain.

FEELINGS CAUSED BY EATING DISORDERS

Keep in mind that one of the main reasons an eating disorder begins is to help make people feel better when life is tough. They feel shame over the behavior, which they have kept secret—and they have to keep their behavior secret so that they can't be stopped. It's one big painful cycle, isn't it?

There's intense anxiety over the process itself, too. Here's how a person with anxiety lives: She constantly thinks about food—how many calories, how many fat grams, how much exercise do you need to do if you eat a cookie? How many times do you check the scale?

She constantly attempts to try to control eating because of the fear of gaining weight. Often meals are avoided or eaten very slowly, fearing that surely it will make her fat. These thoughts begin to control a person's mind 24 hours a day, seven days a week. Imagine your entire life centered on this one issue, depriving you of enjoying friends, fun, and family.

She becomes disgusted with herself, depressed, or very guilty after overeating or missing a weigh-in. Because of her own feelings about herself, as well as because of likely hormone imbalances, she becomes moody and irritable and responds to confrontation and even low-key interchanges with tears, tantrums, or withdrawal.

Eating disorders feel lonely. People with eating disorders pull away from those who care. They often feel they don't fit in anywhere, and even when they do spend time with others, they hold themselves apart. They tend to try to please everyone and withdraw when they inevitably fail. One way of keeping their distance is to either be the caretaker who doesn't need to show weakness, or to be tough and independent and reject all efforts to help.

Whether their disorder is of the starvation type or the bingeing/purging type, it takes up so much physical and emotional energy that they don't have energy or focus to be in serious relationships or even friendships. Those with anorexia tend to be so rigidly controlling that others may not be able to connect with them. Those with bulimia tend to be impulsive and get themselves into difficult situations with people, money, and work. So in addition to their compulsions and obsessions, they feel socially isolated. It's hardly an easy way to live!

Sometimes people who don't realize that they may have an eating disorder can identify with a lot of the feelings that people with

How Are You Feeling?

How many of these emotional situations do you experience?

▸ Intense fear of gaining weight or becoming fat

▸ Problems with drugs, alcohol, sexual activity, or crime

▸ Preoccupation with body weight

▸ Depression or mood swings

▸ Feelings of fatness

▸ Depression with social withdrawal

▸ Uncontrollable fear of inability to stop eating

▸ Feeling misunderstood

▸ Feeling isolated

▸ Inability to relax if unable to exercise

▸ Angry and irritable

▸ Always unhappy with self

▸ Would rather be dead than overweight

Anyone who experiences more than a few of those feelings and behaviors, on more than an occasional basis, needs to seriously consider the possibility that he or she may need professional help. This person needs to consult a doctor or a qualified counselor to prevent more serious problems. This questionnaire can serve as a starting point for a conversation with a professional.

anorexia, bulimia, and binge eating disorders experience. The specific behaviors are often really expressions of their feelings, so anyone who shares these feelings may want to look closely for any patterns of disordered eating.

Physical discomfort. There's often such focus on the big issues of eating disorders that we forget that people live with constantly queasy stomachs, constant diarrhea, bad tastes in the mouth, and headaches, as well as fatigue.

Changes in the mouth are often physical signs of an eating disorder. Malnutrition can cause decay, and erosion of the teeth is caused by stomach acid from vomiting.

Sometimes people turn to alcohol and drugs, simply for relief from the day-to-day stress of maintaining their eating disorders. And those habits cause even further discomfort.

When you read about the feelings associated with eating disorders, you can understand why it's important for people living with anorexia, bulimia, and other disorders to have people like them with whom they can share their experiences and feelings. It's also critical for them to get professional help.

GETTING A DIAGNOSIS

One common characteristic of people with eating disorders is a strong reluctance to seek help—including seeing a physician. But if you suspect that some of the descriptions or feelings might apply to you (even if you don't think you have a full-blown eating disorder), you can see that these disorders are probably too powerful to deal with yourself. People who are in the midst of an eating disorder, or simply in the midst of worrying about whether they have an eating disorder, might not be able to see the symptoms clearly.

It's best to find professional advice for a clear diagnosis. *Diagnose* simply means to identify a condition and differentiate it from other conditions. A diagnosis offers a shorthand way of talking about a particular kind of eating disturbance.

Types of professionals who can diagnose eating disorders include physicians, psychologists, dietitians, and mental-health counselors in private practice or as part of a clinic or treatment center. Professional associations can guide you toward a professional. Here are some valuable Web sites:

➤ American Academy of Child and Adolescent Psychiatry: http://www.aacap.org

> American Dietetic Association: http://www.eatright.org
> National Eating Disorders Association: http://www.national eatingdisorders.org
> National Institute of Mental Health: http://www.nimh.nih.gov

Check with your doctor or another responsible adult. If you have a good relationship with your physician, that's a good place to start, but sometimes it takes a while to come clean with someone you may not have been completely honest with. And sometimes your doctor may not be enough of an expert in the specialized diagnosis you need. You can call a local hospital for a list—and doing that by phone protects your privacy. Medical practitioners usually have referral lists for those seeking counseling help, and they can point you to a source for specialized counseling in eating disorders.

You can ask a physician: "How long have you been in this specialty? Do you work with others as a team? What's your feeling about medications? How do you decide when a person is well? Can I call you any time?

You can ask a counselor: What kind of license or training do you have? How long have you been in this specialty? Do you work with others as a team? Do you prefer medication or not? How long does it take to get an appointment?

A professional should be happy to answer questions like that, and it's up to you to decide if you're comfortable with the answers or the approach. If the physician or counselor doesn't seem like a good fit, keep looking. Or ask him or her for names of other doctors who would be qualified. The hardest part is taking the first step, making contact with a responsible adult, asking the first questions. Sometimes people with eating disorders are afraid that turning to a professional will make them lose control, so it's important to remember that you need help and advice about a different approach.

To make a diagnosis, a good, professional counselor will involve you in a thorough evaluation process. This is confidential. The process may include both medical evaluation and psychological evaluation.

Medical evaluation. A thorough evaluation will begin with a medical exam. Even if you start with a nonmedical counselor, you should be sure to get a checkup. The physical will include the normal exam procedures, as well as a check for dehydration, and functions of the heart and other internal organs. The doctor may refer you to a dentist for possible damage to teeth, especially if your condition includes purging, since stomach acid can damage teeth.

Psychological evaluation. A mental health professional will take a history of your eating patterns and any treatment that you have received in the past. You may be asked to report what you eat in a day (or over several days). You can expect questions about how you view your body and what your attitudes are toward eating. The counselor may use a questionnaire or other techniques to evaluate your mood and anxiety level. A good interview will also look for any triggers for your disordered eating. You will probably be asked about problems that have come up in past relationships.

It's important to be as honest as you can be with these professionals. If they are truly experienced in dealing with possible eating disorders, they will understand how hard they are to talk about. But getting your concerns into the open, in private, is the only way to relieve your worries. The counselor and the physician, along with a dietitian and anyone else involved, can then consult and come up with a diagnosis and any treatment they recommend.

You should expect this kind of thorough approach to your condition. You can expect caring and respectful treatment from them—and remember, they have dealt with many cases of eating disorders and are not there to make judgments.

The very fact that it takes a team of specialists to deal with eating disorders underscores how complex they can be. So far this book has tried to explain and explore the complexity, and to offer clues to understanding it. Eating disorders are not only complicated, though—they are also very dangerous. Following up on clues to a possible disorder is critical. Eating disorders are not something kids have to deal with just because they're teens. And they aren't something kids just grow out of. They are so dangerous that some kids don't get a chance to "grow out of them."

WHAT YOU NEED TO KNOW

- ▶ Eating disorders often stem from emotional and psychological conflicts.
- ▶ Eating disorders go far beyond simple diets.
- ▶ Eating disorders require professional diagnosis and treatment.

5

Dangers of Eating Disorders

Teens go on diets and exercise programs to be slimmer and look better. And they pursue tough food plans as a way to take control of their lives and show their strength. The trouble is, the eating disorders that twist out of these diet plans actually turn on the dieters: It's the eating pattern that ends up weakening the dieter.

Eating disorders are in fact often ways to deal with buried emotions. But the emotional trauma that develops as a result of eating disorders can be much harder to recover from than digging up those buried emotions in the first place. It may not seem to make sense, but then, a lot about eating disorders doesn't make "sense"—especially since eating disorders are so dangerous—but kids get involved with them anyway.

In this chapter you can check out all the harm—physical, mental, social, even appearance—that eating disorders can do, and why they're especially risky for teens. If you see or experience any of the conditions you'll read about in this chapter, take it as seriously as a fire alarm. These danger signs mean treatment is needed—and the earlier treatment begins, the better the outcome, so it's important to read the signals quickly.

KILLER DIETS

People can die from eating disorders. Different studies note the mortality rate ranges from 4 to 10 percent for anorexia, about 10 times the expected mortality rate for a healthy population. Deaths from

How Starvation Works

When the body doesn't get enough fuel from food that's eaten, it starts breaking down fat and muscle to use for the energy it needs to keep vital internal systems functioning, like the heart and the nerves. Vitamins and minerals, which serve to help the nerves and hormones function and to send messages throughout the body, decrease, and the body's organ systems stop working right. The heart is especially affected without needed chemicals to regulate it, and the immune system, which protects the body from disease, also breaks down. At some point, the combination of weakened organs with the nonfunctioning of vital systems causes the body to stop working, and it dies.

bulimia are unusual but happen as a result of electrolyte imbalances and heart complications. The emotional conflicts that contribute to and then result from eating disorders can lead to suicide. The stress on the body from abnormal eating patterns—including purging—can cause heart attacks. Starvation happens when the body is deprived of nutrition long enough to go through chemical changes that may be difficult to reverse.

The death rate for anorexia is higher than that caused by any other mental illness—and anyone who doubts that it is a mental illness just needs to consider that people follow these destructive patterns while being unable to see that they are endangering themselves.

PHYSICAL CONSEQUENCES

Eating disorders are harmful in a variety of physical ways, especially to teens.

Lifelong limits. "Life threatening" doesn't mean only fatal—it means it can threaten your ability to live and grow. It may not seem fair, but the fact is that teenagers, who are the most vulnerable to develop eating disorders, are also the group more likely to be most damaged by them, because their bodies are developing.

(continues on page 48)

Think Again!

Do you believe any of these myths about disordered eating?

- ▶ *You can't die from bulimia.*
- ▶ *If you just start eating, you won't die from anorexia.*
- ▶ *I can make my own choices.*
- ▶ *Overeating can't hurt you.*
- ▶ *It's only a diet.*
- ▶ *Laxatives are natural, right?*
- ▶ *As long as I don't use pills I'm okay.*
- ▶ *Drinking water can keep me in balance.*
- ▶ *Exercise builds up my energy.*

Let's look at the facts.

- ▶ *You can't die from bulimia.* Fact: Bulimia can kill in various ways, and purging is especially dangerous and can cause fatal heart problems.

- ▶ *If you just start eating, you won't die from anorexia.* Fact: If someone could "just start eating," she wouldn't be anorexic. More important, because anorexia is about a lot more than food, it's difficult to get someone to eat more. Finally, anorexia's self-starvation can damage the body's systems so severely that it can't get back on track.

- ▶ *I can make my own choices.* Fact: Because of changes in the brain associated with undernourishment, binge eating, and purging, the person does not, and perhaps cannot, weigh priorities, make judgments, and make choices that are logical and rational for normal people. The part of the brain affected is also the part that is last to develop in adolescence, so judgment may be affected.

- ▶ *Overeating can't hurt you.* Fact: Overeating usually does damage more slowly than other disorders, but it can result in long-term health problems from heart trouble and diabetes to arthritis. It can hurt more quickly, too. Bulimia nervosa patients— even those of normal weight—can severely damage their bodies by frequent binge eating and purging. In rare instances, binge eating causes the stomach to rupture; purging may result in heart failure due to loss of vital electrolytes like potassium.

▸ *It's only a diet.* Fact: Digestion is a complex process affecting every organ, including the brain. Dieting may throw the body out of balance, and may actually cause an increase in weight, which can lead to more intense dieting, which can contribute to the development of an eating disorder.

▸ *Laxatives are natural, right?* Fact: Some foods and plant products act as "natural" laxatives. Being natural doesn't matter. People with eating disorders abuse laxatives because they believe they can remove food from their bodies before the calories are absorbed. (They can't.) And laxatives may cause dangerous reactions.

▸ *As long as I don't use pills I'm okay.* Fact: Wrong! Pills may add to the dangers of dieting, and they can make eating disorders much worse. That does not mean that any weight-control technique that doesn't use pills is safe—they may be risky.

▸ *Drinking water can keep me in balance.* Fact: Not completely. Regular intake of water is good for everyone's health. But when laxatives, enemas, and vomiting remove needed fluids and *electrolytes* from the body, and starving doesn't provide enough fluids, the resulting dehydration and electrolyte imbalance can lead to tremors, weakness, blurry vision, fainting spells, kidney damage, and in some cases death. Drinking water alone won't counteract that. Severe dehydration requires medical treatment. Best not to get dehydrated!

▸ *Exercise builds up my energy.* Fact: To a point, regular, well-managed exercise can build up stamina and can develop muscles, lungs, and heart to allow for comfortable living. But overexercise in a compulsive fashion can cause many of the same kinds of problems as food deprivation.

(continued from page 45)

People who develop anorexia before adulthood may not grow to their full size, and low levels of essential hormones can limit healthy development, including the healthy development of the ability to have children. Even after recovery and weight restoration, a person may not catch up to expected normal height. Poor nutrition may retard the growth of essential bone structure, and weaker bones are easier to break. During high-growth periods of adolescence, broken bones may not heal properly, and the weakened bone mass may never recover.

Other long-term physical consequences: The level of female hormones in the blood of an anorectic woman falls drastically, resulting in delayed sexual development. Her heart rate and blood pressure may drop dangerously low, and loss of potassium in the blood may cause irregular heart rhythms. Her muscles atrophy or waste away, resulting in weakness and loss of muscle function. When a young, growing body has to deal with these kind of ongoing physical threats, it can't develop properly.

Brain damage. Starvation can lead to poor brain function, which muddles thinking and makes dealing with the facts that much more of a challenge. Changes in brain structure and function are early signs of the condition, and it affects teens more than others, since the portion affected is the part that's still under development. In some patients, the brain shrinks, which may affect personality and mood. Most of these changes are directly due to starvation, and may be reversed after normal weight is regained.

Just plain discomfort. Dangerous as the disorders may be, they are also uncomfortable. Dehydration causes excessive thirst and constipation, and reduced body fat leads to lowered body temperature and the inability to withstand cold. Anorectics also experience anemia, swollen joints, reduced muscle mass, and lightheadedness. Insomnia and an antsy restlessness can make them feel jittery—and fatigue can mean that daily life is a drag.

Troublesome and unpredictable as menstrual periods can be for teen girls, they can become extremely irregular and even disappear due to starvation or overexercise. And that is not a good thing—it's a sign that normal development of their reproductive system is just not happening.

Looking good and feeling good. People get involved in eating disorders because they want to "look good." Here are some of the impacts on appearance from eating disorders.

From the effects of bulimia, we see:

> Unusual swelling of the cheeks or jaw area—"chipmunk cheeks"—due to salivary-gland damage from vomiting.
> Calluses on the back of the hands and knuckles from self-induced vomiting.
> Discoloration or staining of the teeth.

In the extreme phase of anorexia, we see:

> Emaciated body.
> Dry, blotchy skin that has a gray or yellow tone.
> Brittle nails and hair.
> Limbs often covered with a fine, downy hair called *lanugo.*

Both starving and vomiting can lead to bad breath.

Here's what one girl saw in the mirror after living with an eating disorder for a while: "I was in horrible shape. I had absolutely no color in my face and resembled a ghost. My skin had turned a bizarre yellowish-purple color. My teeth were yellow and rotten from the acid that shot up into my mouth during daily purges. I shook uncontrollably from malnutrition. My hair was falling out in handfuls."

People with eating disorders tend to wear layered, loose-fitting clothes in order to conceal the changing shape of their bodies. In addition, their sex hormones may decrease, leading to less interest in sex.

Plus, those who starve or purge to lose weight need to take in another surprising fact—eating disorders can actually increase someone's weight. Research shows that a diet is almost guaranteed to lead to a gain in weight, because of the body's natural reaction to deprivation. The "yo-yo" effect can be the body's natural attempt to get back on an even keel.

Well, does all this effort at least make a person sexy? All those folks on TV are skinny *and* attractive. In real life, though, an over-dieting person's sex drive usually goes down.

IT'S ENOUGH TO MAKE YOU SICK

To review: Eating disorders can kill you and harm your appearance. They can also make you sick, sometimes dangerously so. Here are some examples:

> Dangerously high or low blood pressure, depending on whether the disorder is starving or gorging type
> Elevated cholesterol levels

- Heart disease
- Type 2 diabetes
- Gallbladder disease
- Nerve damage
- Seizures
- Digestive problems
- Teeth and gum erosion
- Malnutrition
- Dehydration
- Ruptured stomach
- Kidney and liver damage
- Tears of the esophagus

Every organ of the body—not just the "fat"—is affected by disordered eating, so every organ, including teeth and hair, can be damaged, often for the long term.

THE SOCIAL BACKFIRE

One reason people are vulnerable to developing an eating disorder has to do with gaining approval of their families and wanting to be attractive to friends. Like so much else related to eating disorders, these nonphysical aspects backfire, too.

- Eating disorders can disrupt family life as conflicts arise over food, weight, and treatment.
- Feelings of alienation and loneliness only increase as the sufferer feels, "I don't fit in anywhere."
- Friendships and romantic relationships may become damaged or destroyed. The person with the eating disorder may become emotionally cold and withdrawn, crabby and cranky, and secretive and controlling, as her focus narrows to her own preoccupations.

More bad feelings. As painful as the medical consequences of an eating disorder are, the psychological agony can be just as painful, believing that weight loss will improve self-esteem, self-confidence, and happiness. In fact, persistent undereating, binge eating, and purging have the opposite effect. Eating-disordered individuals typically struggle with one or more of the following complications: depression, low self-esteem, shame and guilt, mood swings, and perfectionism.

DANGEROUS PROCESSES

For all the dangerous and often unplanned effects of disorders, the techniques themselves are dangerous. For instance, while bulimia doesn't lead to starvation in the same way as anorexia does, the processes it employs are very harmful.

Although some people who have bulimia may look "healthier" than people who have anorexia, bingeing and purging create potentially serious physical problems in addition to depriving the body of nutrition. The hazards include damage to the teeth, throat, esophagus, and stomach, due to the effects of acid in the vomit. More serious results may include stomach ruptures due to bingeing, and heart failure due to the loss of vital electrolytes, such as sodium and potassium, through purging. When *emetics* are used to induce vomiting, these effects are intensified; and the use of laxatives can lead to a dependence on them that makes regular bowel movements nearly impossible.

What is purging about? Purging is thought to control weight. But it can serve other "purposes." Purging may act as a release for negative emotions, like anger, and purgers may feel like they are ridding themselves of uncomfortable feelings. Some people get more relief from the purging behavior than from bingeing. It can be powerfully reinforcing. Some people believe it can protect them from weight gain, and free them from restricted eating. Even though it's potentially dangerous, it may give people a temporary sense of self-control. Types of purging include:

▸ Self-induced vomiting. People may use an emetic to induce vomiting or use something to make themselves gag. After a while, many bulimics simply bend over the toilet and are able to vomit spontaneously. Vomiting generally produces a further breakdown in control over food intake.

▸ Laxatives. Stimulant laxatives flush out the large colon. However, most calories are already absorbed in the small intestine, making it an ineffective way to lose weight. Frequent use of laxatives may decrease bowel effectiveness.

▸ Obsessive exercise. Many people will work out for hours in the gym, to "burn off" the food they've eaten. This kind of exercise can be dangerous, too. Not only does it put someone at risk for injury, but it creates the same kind of biological imbalances in the body that starvation does, including stopping girls' menstrual periods.

DANGEROUS SUBSTANCES

According to some reports, between 3.5 and 7 percent of high school students abuse laxatives. Between 40 and 75 percent of bulimics abuse laxatives and about 15 percent of bulimics may abuse laxatives more than once a day. Almost 30 percent of bulimic patients use emetics, with 10 percent of those abusing them regularly.

Yet these are not effective weight loss methods! It is difficult to purge everything ingested, and some calories will be absorbed before vomiting. The use of laxatives also doesn't reduce calorie intake, as laxatives clear the large intestine, which is the last part of the digestive system, not the small intestine where nutrients actually enter the body.

Laxative abuse is not only an inefficient manner of promoting weight loss, it is also dangerous. Individuals lose water, not weight, and it is a false belief that laxatives will diminish calorie absorption. Instead, laxative abusers can develop life-threatening medical complications:

▸ The colon stops functioning properly and may require surgery.
▸ They fail to absorb important vitamins.
▸ Diarrhea may cause electrolyte imbalances.
▸ Potassium, magnesium, and other electrolytes are lost, causing arrhythmias, muscle cramps, or seizures.
▸ Laxative abusers are faced with periods of constipation (because they need the laxatives to move their bowels) and diarrhea.
▸ When they try to stop they may gain water weight and return to the use of laxatives.

Emetics. Emetics are chemicals designed to produce vomiting in case of emergencies, like swallowing poison. They are very dangerous when used for any other purpose. They can cause fatal damage to the heart. Yet people purge by forcing vomiting this way.

Diuretics. Water pills have no effect on calories or body fat, but "water weight" is reduced. Diuretics throw electrolytes, those chemicals that make for proper bodily functions, out of kilter, which can be deadly.

Diet pills. Diet pills may be toxic if taken in high numbers.

Herbal products. People often think herbal products are safe because they are natural. This is not true. Herbal products are not regulated by the Food and Drug Administration (FDA) and therefore do not need to prove they are effective or safe. Many of them are just as dangerous as chemical products.

Eating disorders create a destructive, frustrating cycle. When you use chemicals like diuretics, laxatives, emetics, and pills, you raise its danger level *without* creating diet "success." This is a self-maintaining cycle: starting with low self-esteem, to concerns about weight, to increase in dieting, to more severe dieting, to loss of control/bingeing, to purging. Dieting may lead to bingeing, which leads to less self-esteem and more concerns about weight and more dieting. Bingeing may lead to purging, undercutting self-esteem. Purging can lead to people feeling hungry again, which leads to more bingeing. The emetics may make the bingeing more severe, just as the laxatives and the diuretics cause a weight-gain counteraction.

To repeat: Purging rarely works well for weight loss. Laxatives and diuretics make you lose water, not weight. Vomiting is ineffective, since well over half of the calories have already been absorbed.

If people don't die in the process, they're trapped into a long-term cycle of danger.

UNBALANCED DIETS DON'T WORK

If unbalanced diets don't work, why are they advertised on TV and promoted in magazines and Internet pop-ups? Because people happily spend money on diet products in the hope that they'll become slim and beautiful. But here are the facts:

> Research shows that 95 percent of all diets fail. No matter how hard we may try, our bodies aren't made for deprivation. It's likely that they are designed to maintain a certain weight range.
> A 2006 study of college-age women showed that dieting actually predicted weight *gain.*
> We often gain back more weight than we lost, because when we restrict our diets so much that we are consistently hungry, the effect is for us to gorge when we finally allow ourselves to eat. In the long term, this often means gaining back more weight than we lost.
> Even more, dieting decreases the body's rate of *metabolism,* because the body believes that it needs to conserve what it takes in.
> When someone with an eating disorder breaks a diet, he feels so guilty that he works even harder at dieting, which leads to more hunger, and so the cycle repeats again and again.

A healthier approach that is more effective in treatment programs is to avoid letting yourself get over-hungry. Instead of starving and bingeing, eating smaller amounts of healthy food on a regular basis is what works to regulate weight and to develop healthier eating habits.

HOW TO PROTECT YOURSELF FROM THE DANGERS OF EATING DISORDERS

Prevention begins with awareness. This section has focused on raising your awareness of not only the dangers of eating disorders but also of the warning signals, including the signs of disordered eating.

The next section focuses on how to deal with these dangerous disorders. It's especially important to be aware of some other facts: Eating disorders are treatable, and people do recover from them. So learning of the dangers or the threat of them should encourage someone to seek treatment, not give up and sink into despair. Sooner is better than later. The sooner someone begins treatment, the sooner he or she can develop a new and positive life.

WHAT YOU NEED TO KNOW

- ▶ Early intervention can improve chances for a healthy life.
- ▶ The effects of eating disorders can be physically devastating.
- ▶ The patterns and processes of all eating disorders backfire, so that they may actually cause weight gain, lack of control, and unhappiness.

6

Recognizing Eating Disorders

Obtaining treatment for an eating disorder is critical to restoring a person to health or even saving a life, so it may seem puzzling that it's so hard to get people into treatment. The reasons for that can be seen as part of the disorder itself. Often those with eating disorders—and their families—are in denial about it: They may not want to see that there is a problem. Also, people with eating disorders protect their habits. They have a huge and irrational emotional investment in not changing their eating behaviors and in keeping them secret. Getting past those barriers of denial and secrecy becomes key to recovery, because the earlier the diagnosis, the earlier the intervention, the more successful the treatment.

POWER OF DENIAL

Denial may not make sense to outsiders, but for sufferers it is a very powerful psychological tool used unconsciously to protect themselves from painful reality. It's not just that someone may refuse to see odd eating habits as a disorder—someone may also be using the eating disorder itself to deny a problem in other areas of life. If family troubles are causing turmoil, for example, food can become something to focus on and control instead.

Denial may be playing a role in those around a person with an eating disorder as well. Family members may just not want to see the problem, so they convince themselves there is no problem. Denial is made even easier when the person with the disorder seems to have everything else going well in her life. Many people who have eating disorders seem to be in complete control of their lives. A parent whose child is getting good grades, is active in extracurricular activities, and is tidy and polite would understandably have a hard time admitting there was anything wrong. But of all the potential threats to someone with an eating disorder, the worst may be denial, since it slows access to treatment. This means that those close to someone with an eating disorder need to be able to recognize it and step in as necessary.

SYSTEM OF SECRETS

Denial is not the only powerful psychological force for hiding eating disorders. It's also true that people with eating disorders often work hard to keep the problem hidden. They keep their disordered patterns secret because the disorder is not so much about food, eating, and diets, as one teen in recovery puts it, but more about finding ways to escape painful feelings. Food is easier to control and manage than feelings, another says, and then the bad feelings that come from the eating problems also have to be covered up. To reveal the disorder means having to deal with those feelings, like anxiety, depression, and anger.

People with eating disorders often seem desperate to cling to them, no matter how physically destructive they are. Perhaps only someone "inside" an eating disorder can fully understand this intense psychological drive. If they are forced to give up their disordered eating, they would have to face what they don't want to. Maybe a family situation causes them pain. Or they may fear growing up itself. Since anorexia does slow development in girls and can cause menstrual periods to stop in women, they can stay like "little girls" who don't have to deal with the problems of the world. This is not likely to be a conscious decision, but professionals learn that it is often an unconscious motivation when a young woman feels safer staying a child.

Powerful feelings. A whole set of new feelings can develop during the course of a disorder itself. People with eating disorders describe a sense of both shame and pride. They may feel that they are "not good enough"—a feeling that self-criticism reinforces. One teen explains online: "The voices of our eating disorders also convince us we have no willpower, that we are weak when we've eaten, and that no one will ever love us. They harass us with guilt and even berate us for the eating disorder behavior itself. It is no wonder recovery is so difficult and such hard work. We are battling with ourselves over what we are convinced we deserve (and that our negative voices keep reminding us of) as opposed to what we truly do deserve (recovery, happiness, and self-love!).”

Those with eating disorders may also feel pride over being able to accomplish what others can't—to be thinner than anyone else, to exercise more, to “be perfect.” This pride exists in the false sense of control they have over themselves—and over others, especially their parents. One girl talks about how she puts her mother down by calling her “just a worrier.” Non-eating can be an effective way to control one's parents, for whom feeding is a prime concern. It's one area where kids of any age can “take charge,” since it may be difficult to convince them to eat.

HIDING OUT

Eating disorders cause people to isolate themselves. They need privacy to practice the behaviors, whether bingeing, purging, or weighing. Then the isolation itself becomes part of the disorder. The pattern becomes so strong that it's even harder to break. They may isolate themselves to avoid people who comment about their appearance, whether overly skinny or suddenly heavy, and who might make them more likely to try to stop the disorder. It's hard for them to be in social situations involving food, so they stay away.

Some people with eating disorders, especially in isolation, call the disorder their “friend.” This “friend” has been what helped them handle frightening emotions. It's what has kept them company when others have lost interest in them. So letting someone else in on their secret is like turning on a friend.

The disorder serves so many powerful functions that people work hard to hide their disease. In order to hide the fact that they don't eat, some even eat. Some doctors can't even tell that they have a disorder. Many women can maintain a near-normal weight because their metabolism has slowed down so much that they need very few calories to live. Others employ dangerous tactics like *water loading* before weigh-ins. They drink huge quantities of water to fool the doctors, nurses, therapists, and the scale.

READING THE SIGNS

Being able to read the signs of eating disorders is the first step toward finding treatment for a loved one. It might seem that, in their extreme forms, some of these disorders should be fairly easy to notice—a skeletal-looking body (the result of extreme weight loss), obvious signs of vomiting and diarrhea, hours spent each day at the gym, and so on.

But many eating disorders don't reach these extreme stages, and often there are other factors that hide the telltale signs.

Disordered dieting. "Cultural thinness" means that, since it's okay to be slim, it takes sharp eyes to see who is *too* thin. People with anorexia may not receive medical or psychological attention until they have already become dangerously thin and malnourished.

Who Could Have an Eating Disorder?

Which of the following has an eating disorder? Someone who . . .

1. often vomits, but doesn't lose weight?
2. exercises long and hard?
3. seems very shy?
4. is a bodybuilder?
5. eats only organic foods?
6. eats only at night?

Answer: All of the above may be aspects of what is considered "disordered eating." Though anorexia and bulimia are the only medically recognized disorders, there are others called EDNOS—"eating disorders not otherwise specified." They include:

1. purging disorder
2. anorexia athletica (compulsive exercising)
3. body dysmorphic disorder (BDD): Excessively concerned about appearance, and feel so ugly they act shy
4. muscle dysmorphic disorder (bigorexia): Wants bigger muscles
5. *orthorexia nervosa*: Eats only certain foods and feels superior to "normal eaters"
6. night-eating syndrome and sleep-related eating disorder

The consequences of "normal," or socially approved, dieting can resemble anorexia or bulimia in milder forms. Researchers at the University of Toronto found that people who go on diets tend to eat like "starving" people—they deprive themselves for as long as they can and then end up gorging on food—in other words, to act like people with true eating disorders and thus make the real ones harder to identify. Also, people with bulimia are often normal weight and are able to hide their illness from others for years because they don't get too skinny.

Dieting itself ("normal" and disordered) can take many forms: for example, avoiding eating for long periods of time (in other words, starving, which may lead to bingeing); avoiding eating certain types of food (craving may lead to bingeing); and restricting the total amount of food eaten (starving, which may lead to bingeing). Each type illustrates an unhealthy approach to nourishing the body. There are different levels of dieting, from casual to obsessive. For example, the "chronic dieter" keeps careful track of foods selected from a limited list, focusing on those that will help "lose weight" and avoiding those that might cause weight gain. Chronic dieters conscientiously exercise at least once or twice a day and weigh daily, but they can stop this pattern, and often do, even when they hope to lose more weight.

Or, someone may have "disordered" approaches to food that aren't severe enough to qualify as eating disorders. For instance, they may eat only "low-calorie" foods, or eat only once a day, and weigh themselves frequently.

Finally, true eating disorders involve *obsessive-compulsive behaviors.* That is, sufferers experience a *compulsion*—an irresistible inner urge—to commit an irrational act, and are fueled by an *obsession*—a persistent, unshakable idea that repeats again and again. People for whom dieting becomes an obsession can't stop.

You can't always tell by looking that an adolescent is struggling with an eating issue. Overweight teens sometimes take the drastic and unhealthy step of using laxatives to try to lose weight. Or, they may eat, but only certain foods. Someone who has an incredibly strict eating regimen may not lose weight because he gets enough calories to maintain it. The following are the classic signs of eating disorders:

Anorexia nervosa. Deliberate self-starvation with weight loss is the key feature of anorexia. Fueled by an intense, persistent fear of gaining weight, they engage in continuous dieting, refusing to eat at all or rigidly restricting what they will eat. They often exercise compulsively as well, to burn up the few calories they may take in.

They are preoccupied with food, calories, nutrition, and/or cooking, and know exactly how much they're taking in and how much they're burning up. They weigh themselves frequently and can often tell to the ounce how much they weigh. People with anorexia do not, however, have such a clear idea of how they look: Their bodies can look like skeletons, but the reflection they see in the mirror looks to them to be "too fat." If a girl wears size two, she's not happy till she's in size one.

This lack of realistic self-perception is often accompanied by a strong tendency to isolate from family and friends, especially those who might criticize their weight loss. They prefer to eat alone, as well, and in that way have more control over their intake. The urge to persist in dieting is so strong that they may allow themselves to eat more than they'd like in order to conceal their true situation.

Their weight will continue to drop, however, and they will exhibit other physical symptoms as well. The lack of food changes the hormone balance in their bodies, so girls will stop having menstrual periods, or delay starting menstruation if they haven't already started. They may develop unusual face or body hair, called lanugo, associated with hormonal imbalances. Because their bodies aren't receiving enough calories to produce heat, they may feel cold all the time.

Bulimia nervosa. People with bulimia "binge and purge." That is, they eat a lot, then throw it up, use laxatives to cause diarrhea, exercise obsessively to burn calories, or all three. They also show an unusual preoccupation with food: They may or may not "diet," but they do focus a lot of time and attention on details of shopping, cooking, and eating. They may isolate themselves because they usually do their binge eating in secret. It's also common for them to "disappear" after meals so that they can vomit up what they have eaten. They may use drugs to induce vomiting, or gag themselves with their fingers after eating to throw up. Reddened fingers from induced vomiting are one physical sign of bulimia. They may have a lot of heartburn or problems with the throat or esophagus caused by vomited stomach acid. People with bulimia also often have irregular menstrual periods, since bodily hormones are thrown out of balance by the eating disorder.

Dental evidence. The teeth show another physical problem common among people with eating disorders. Bulimia can damage teeth. The stomach acid from vomiting can eat the enamel, resulting in increased sensitivity to temperature. In extreme cases the pulp can

Common Misconceptions about Eating Disorders

It's easier to recognize eating disorders when you can clear away some misconceptions about them.

> ▶ *Eating disorders are a sign of shame.* Fact: Eating disorders are not due to a failure of will or behavior; rather, they are real, treatable medical illnesses in which certain maladaptive patterns of eating take on a life of their own.

> ▶ *Eating disorders affect only women.* Fact: Females are more likely than males to develop an eating disorder, but EDs are not exclusive to women. An estimated 5–15 percent of people with anorexia or bulimia and an estimated 35 percent of those with binge-eating disorders are male.

> ▶ *Eating disorders are a fad or just a phase people grow out of.* Fact: EDs are a serious illness that require the earliest intervention possible.

> ▶ *It's the troubled kids who have eating problems.* Fact: Anyone can suffer from an eating disorder.

be exposed and cause infection, discoloration, or even pulp death (death of a tooth that may require extraction). Bulimia can also lead to enlargement of the salivary glands; dry mouth; reddened, dry, cracked lips; and tooth decay, which can actually be aggravated by extensive toothbrushing or rinsing following vomiting.

Less well known is that people with anorexia have dental trouble, too. Their saliva is deficient in the buffers that protect teeth from the effects of acid manufactured by bacteria in the mouth, and that are present in food and soft drinks. Normal saliva contains buffers that are made in part from materials found in fatty foods.

With the prevalence of over-the-counter "teeth whiteners," the dental clues can be harder to see. But an unusual obsession with the teeth can be a sign of some kind of food compulsion. Poor teeth, isolation, carefully managed eating, a certain sense of being better than other people: These are the kind of clues that call attention to an eating disorder.

Personality traits. People with eating disorders show some characteristic personality styles and behaviors. Anorexia and other deprivation disorders may be part of a pattern that is extremely controlled and controlling. Those with bulimia or binge-eating disorders may display extreme emotional ups and downs. When combined with other clues, these traits should be warning signs. Here's how one patient describes herself:

> I could never see myself letting go of the "control" I had over my life, others' lives and their feelings, and controlling what I put into my body. Keeping my weight down made everything so much more manageable and bearable. If I let go and relaxed about everything I obsessed about and stopped trying to fix everything in the universe, my life was worth nothing. Molehills were mountains. I caused people to have upset in their lives; I don't deserve to enjoy a meal, or anything for that matter, because someone else was worse off than I. I must not be happy as others aren't.

Other clues. People with eating disorders may have substance-abuse problems as well, or they may be in recovery from a substance-abuse problem and have "switched addictions." An addict comments:

> My food stuff really didn't come up until I got clean. Drugs and alcohol had stopped working. I went into treatment, I got out and I was clean. But I crossed over from not using drugs and alcohol to using food to suppress my emotions. I was real clear I wasn't going to use drugs and alcohol anymore, but I still had all these issues that were unresolved. I needed something to medicate me.

"Cutting" or self-mutilation is another drastic technique kids some individuals use to manage intense emotions, and it can go along with eating disorders, as well.

WHAT'S TOO THIN?

Doctors evaluate fitness by comparing height and weight in a formula resulting in the BMI, or body mass index. A BMI of under 18 is considered underweight. For most people, here's how to determine where you are: Locate your height (without shoes) on the table opposite and

SIGNIFICANTLY UNDERWEIGHT ACCORDING TO HEIGHT (BODY MASS INDEX OF 18)*

Height (inches)	Weight (pounds)	Height (inches)	Weight (pounds)
58	86	68	118
58½	88	68½	120
59	89	69	121
59½	90	69½	124
60	91	70	125
60½	93	70½	127
61	95	71	128
61½	96	71½	131
62	99	72	132
62½	100	72½	134
63	101	73	135
63½	103	73½	138
64	105	74	140
64½	106	74½	141
65	108	75	144
65½	109	75½	146
66	112	76	147
66½	113	76½	149
67	114	77	152
67½	117	77½	154

BMI = (lbs) ÷ (inches) ÷ (inches) x 703

see if your body weight (in light indoor clothing) is below that listed. Interpreting BMI percentiles for children and teens is more complicated because of the difference in body fat that changes with age and between the amount of fat expected to be present in boys and girls. If you are in the lower fifth percentile, you should definitely speak with your doctor. To calculate body mass index exactly, divide your weight (in pounds) by your height (in inches); divide this again by height in inches and multiply by 703.

(continues on page 66)

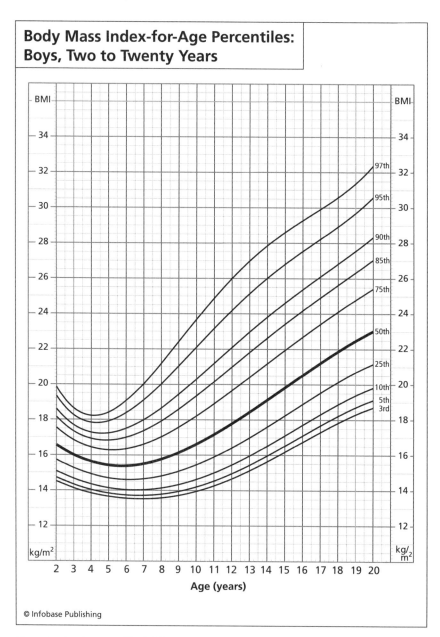

Body Mass Index-for-Age Percentiles: Boys, Two to Twenty Years

Boys in the lowest fifh BMI percentile are considered underweight.

Source: National Center for Health Statistics / National Center for Chronic Disease Prevention and Health Promotion, 2000.

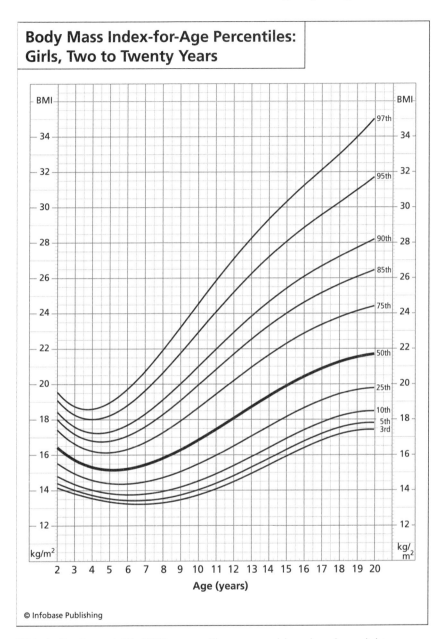

Body Mass Index-for-Age Percentiles: Girls, Two to Twenty Years

© Infobase Publishing

Girls in the lowest fifh BMI percentile are considered underweight.

Source: National Center for Health Statistics / National Center for Chronic Disease Prevention and Health Promotion, 2000.

(continued from page 63)

A MATTER OF LIFE OR DEATH

Eating disorders tend to be progressive—they may get worse because no one can achieve "perfection," so the person keeps trying. Eating disorders can indeed kill those who are afflicted by them, but even if they aren't fatal, they can damage the developing bodies and brains of young people who are starving or otherwise hurting themselves.

The isolation of the disease can also deprive a young person of critical social interactions. And since an eating disorder is often a mask for depression or a cry for help, injury by accidents and even suicide can be an end result of unaddressed eating disorders.

One student who is now almost in full recovery from both anorexia and bulimia says that she thought that sooner or later she would either kill herself purging, or someone would force her into treatment again. As summed up by the National Eating Disorders Association (NEDA): "Dieting, bingeing, and purging help some people cope with their emotions and help them feel in control of their lives. Unchecked, these behaviors weaken physical health, control, and self-esteem. If left untreated, eating disorders can forever alter a life's course and shatter valuable relationships with family and friends." The association emphasizes that early detection of disordered eating habits is one of the most important factors to achieve successful recovery. As NEDA observes, "It's not just about risking death or damaging your organs for life. There's a daily pain that can be almost unendurable: Simply facing the question 'How are you doing?' with a smile and an 'Okay' day after day when everything is anything *but* okay can make someone come to feel that death must be better than another day of the misery."

INTERVENTION

People with eating disorders often do not recognize or admit that they are ill. As a result, they may strongly resist getting and staying in treatment. Family members or other trusted individuals can be helpful in ensuring that the person with an eating disorder receives needed care and rehabilitation. For some people, treatment may be long term. Because eating disorders can have various effects on the body, one way to approach treatment is through specific specialists. Often treatment can begin for just one aspect of the disorder: Someone may go to a dentist because of teeth and mouth problems. It is often the pain and discomfort related to dental complications that first causes patients to consult with a health professional. Dental hygienists and dentists are often the first health professionals to observe signs and symptoms of disordered eating habits. Or the individual may consult a psychiatrist for depression, or a nutritionist for "help with a diet."

The harder people try to hide the signs of their disordered eating, the more important it may be for them to get help. Intervention may be needed. Parents can and should practice intervention simply by sending a minor child in for treatment. A child or teen who isn't thriving needs to see a doctor and can be compelled to go into treatment. Though this may not be the ideal way to start treatment, it may be necessary.

Success is more likely, though, if the patient is involved in the process. Intervention need not be as dramatic and emotionally intense as TV shows depict. One way professionals help a patient move toward choosing treatment is a brief, nonjudgmental interview and feedback session designed to enhance people's motivation to change their behavior. This kind of brief therapy, added to a self-help program, appears to be effective in treating some people with two common types of eating disorders—bulimia nervosa and binge-eating disorder. University of Washington research indicates that a technique called motivational interviewing may be a cost-effective way of providing assistance to a population that is particularly resistant to treatment. It gets the patient from a stage of denial and secrecy toward a willingness to enter treatment.

WHAT YOU NEED TO KNOW

> Denial can keep people from acknowledging an eating disorder in themselves or a loved one.
> People with eating disorders work hard to keep them secret.
> There are clues to eating disorders.
> Since eating disorders are dangerous and potentially fatal, finding treatment as soon as possible is essential.
> Interventions may be needed to get a person into treatment.

7

Treatment for Eating Disorders

Eating disorders start with a diet or with some other shift in eating that becomes a habit, so it might seem that solutions should be just as simple—but they aren't. Treatment requires multiple approaches coordinated among different specialists, and it needs to be adapted to individual situations. Adding to the complexity is the fact that people with eating disorders cling to their disease and feel deep terror of letting it go. The secrecy, isolation, and need for control that characterize eating disorders can combine to make successful treatment a challenge.

Complex as it can be, treatment is made as pleasant as possible. The more people know that, the more open people will be to it. An image of treatment as harsh and rigid may have grown out of earlier approaches to treatment and be reinforced by often highly emotionalized media presentations, as well as rumors spread by the "proanorexia" Web sites. Fears and misconceptions about treatment can create the greatest stumbling blocks, when the fact is that successful therapy is supportive and gradual.

Eating disorders may be pervasive, stubborn, and dangerous, but they are highly treatable. Different individuals and different disorders require specialized treatments. Emergency treatment may be needed for someone whose anorexia has become life-threatening, but the overall goals are the same: Therapy for teens with eating disorders involves helping individuals to address both disordered eating behaviors and thinking, and to develop new patterns of dealing with food. Specific goals include:

1. Restoration of a healthy body weight
2. Development of normal eating behavior
3. Development of social comfort, and nutritional balance in eating situations
4. Treatment of psychiatric disorders related to eating problems
5. Appropriate exercise patterns
6. Restoration of accurate body perceptions and positive sense of identity
7. Treatment of medical complications connected with disorders
8. Improved family/interpersonal relationships
9. Aftercare plans for treatment
10. Relapse-prevention plans and readmission criteria

Eating disorders are illnesses that involve physical, mental, and emotional issues, so treatment must address all those factors, while at the same time restoring the body to health. Specialists who participate include physicians, nurses, and other medical personnel; psychiatrists, family counselors, and other psychotherapists; dietitians and nutritionists; and exercise therapists. Treatment is individualized according to a person's needs and histories, but group activity is also important, to provide peer support and to counteract the isolating effects of eating disorders.

THE TREATMENT PROCESS

The first step in treatment is diagnosis, or assessment. Assessment involves careful diagnosis of the specifics of the disorder (if any), as well as physiological tests and perhaps psychiatric evaluations. Initial interviews may include a question or two about possible eating issues, or the interviewer may ask for a sample of a typical day's intake, from the time the patient gets up till going to bed. If any foods or food groups are excluded, the interviewer may ask why.

A thorough evaluation should include the following:

Medical exam. A thorough evaluation will include a medical exam. If you start by seeing a counselor, for example, the counselor should refer you to a doctor. Expect the doctor to take your vital signs, of course, and your height and weight (this happens during almost any doctor's appointment). You will be checked for appropriate physical growth and development.

The doctor will likely check you for signs of dehydration, since eating disorders often leave the body drained of water. Expect your heart to be checked (especially since heart failure is a frequent cause of death in advanced anorexia). It is common to take a blood sample to get information about whether your body's internal systems are working normally. If you purge, you may be referred to a dentist to have your teeth evaluated for damage from stomach acid.

Psychiatric evaluation. If you don't start by seeing a counselor or psychiatrist, your doctor will probably refer you to one. This person will gather a history of your disordered eating and any treatment that you have received in the past. It is common to provide a report of what you eat in a day (or several days).

You can expect to hear questions about how you view your body and what your attitudes are toward eating. Your mood and anxiety level will be evaluated, since these can fuel eating disorders, and vice versa. You may also be asked whether you have ever suffered abuse. A good interview will also explore any stressors that trigger disordered eating or magnify the effects of the disorder. You will probably be asked about problems that have come up in past relationships.

Next steps. Providers will base their treatment choices on the results of these evaluations. Treatment may involve changes to your diet, counseling, medications, and medical checks. It may occur in an outpatient setting or an inpatient treatment center, depending on the severity of your symptoms.

If it's determined to be necessary, a patient may be hospitalized. There may be a fairly brief emergency stay to get a critically ill patient stabilized, or a longer hospitalization in a specialized facility.

But each treatment plan is individualized. For example, someone with occasional purging problems but no physical problems might need an initial checkup with a physician, but then see only a therapist. Or, a stable weight restrictionist may also only need a therapist. Some people need to be encouraged to eat what they're hungry for, and give up food rules. In this case, seeing a nutritionist would be unnecessary. Some may need to see physicians regularly; others rely more on psychiatrists.

Depending on the specifics of the patient's condition, treatment can be successful after a fairly brief series of sessions with a therapist, or it can take longer or require more intense multidisciplinary attention. Most patients find longer-term follow-up valuable—perhaps in the form of professional therapy, or through support groups, or simply by employing techniques learned in the treatment process.

TREATMENT METHODS

A wide range of methods are used in the treatment of eating disorders, separately or in combination. Depending on the patient's condition, treatment can take place in a hospital, an outpatient clinic, a counseling center, or a controlled residential setting. These include medical treatment, individual and group psychotherapy, *family therapy,* nutritional counseling, and pharmacotherapy.

To be effective, each treatment approach includes basic education about the disorder for both patient and family, along the lines of the material presented in the first chapters of this book.

Emergency medical treatment. Though hospitalization is not common, treatment—especially for anorexia—may begin in a hospital, because sometimes the first goal is to stabilize or even save a life. Hospitalization is more common for anorexics than for bulimics and especially for anorexics who purge, since they put themselves in the greatest physical danger. Professionals make a decision to hospitalize a patient for treatment based on an individual's physical and mental condition. Factors considered include amount of weight lost—patients 15–20 percent below healthy weight—especially when combined with speed and persistence of weight loss despite therapy.

Hospitalization is also likely to be necessary in cases where serious physical problems exist, including diabetes and certain heart irregularities, or when mental illness such as depression puts a patient in danger. Lack of response to outpatient treatment programs may also result in hospitalization, as can absence of a helpful home environment.

First level of treatment: Outpatient psychotherapy. Seeing a therapist in his or her office once or twice a week, as part of individual or group treatment, and perhaps including couples or family treatment. Most people can be successfully treated at this least-intensive level of treatment.

Second level of treatment: Day treatment programs. For people who continue with symptoms in spite of outpatient treatment. Day treatment programs involve the individual going to a daylong or sometimes evening-long treatment for one or two meals, group therapy, and possibly family treatment before going home at night. This treatment level offers more ability to help control symptoms than does the first level of treatment. Many people are able to successfully change eating patterns in day treatment programs, which are cheaper and less intrusive than inpatient hospitalization.

Third level of treatment: Inpatient hospitalization. For people
for whom day treatment isn't enough. This involves being admitted to
a hospital for management of eating problems. Some ED programs in
psychiatric hospitals require patients to be medically stable, because
a psychiatric unit often isn't equipped for complicated medical
emergencies, so some may need to be admitted to a medical unit for
stabilization first, then to the ED unit for treatment. These stays can
last anywhere from a week to several months. Because the person is
there around the clock, this allows for most control of symptomatic
behaviors.

Longer-term treatment: Residential treatment. Sometimes,
particularly following an inpatient stay, a person elects residential
treatment. As with inpatient stays, the person lives at a facility, and
continues with monitored eating, group and individual psychotherapy, and educational activities. There is usually more flexibility than
a hospital, and it's more geared toward assisting the person toward
independent living.

Psychotherapy. Psychotherapy can help with eating disorders as
well as the other psychiatric illnesses that frequently occur with
them. Practitioners work with individuals and with groups, and deal
directly with the disorders as well as potential underlying issues.
Eating disorders frequently co-occur with other psychiatric disorders
such as depression, substance abuse, and anxiety disorders. In addition, people who suffer from eating disorders can experience a wide
range of physical health complications, including serious heart conditions and kidney failure, which may lead to death. Recognition of
eating disorders as real and treatable diseases, therefore, is critically
important.

One commonly employed psychological approach to treating eating disorders is *cognitive behavioral therapy,* or CBT. When used with
patients who want to change their eating patterns, CBT may prove
sufficient by itself, but in many cases, at later stages of recovery,
"insight therapies" may be used on a longer term basis. The initial
aim is to improve eating patterns, so the therapist often works with
dietitians and other medical professionals.

CBT is divided into three stages. In stage one, the main emphasis
is on educating the patient about the mechanisms that maintain the
illness, and steps are taken to replace disordered eating with more
regular patterns. In stage two, further emphasis on eating regularly
without dieting is combined with a focus on cognitive procedures,

examining the thoughts, beliefs, and values that maintain the problem. Stage three considers relapse-prevention strategies.

CBT works by addressing emotional triggers and thinking patterns and helping the patient to identify, question, and modify relevant thoughts, beliefs, and attitudes. CBT is usually one-to-one therapy.

Another form of individual psychotherapy that is proving effective with eating disorders: dialectical behavior therapy (DBT). DBT may be especially appropriate for treating binge-eating disorder, because it helps patients regulate the emotional ups and downs that trigger this disordered eating pattern. One basic skill is learning to breathe with focus on the diaphragm, which encourages relaxation. It also includes

One Patient's Experience in Psychotherapy

Here's how psychotherapy worked with a patient who describes herself as "anorexic for six years now." Her anorexia had become dangerous, and once her weight had been stabilized, a professional was able to help her "work backwards" from her unhealthy status to a new understanding:

> I know it was triggered by a relationship gone wrong, the idea that if I lost some weight (I was quite "chubby"), he would care for me again. I lost some weight fast, and the "you look great" comments started. So I felt I was on the right track. To make an already long story short, it didn't win back my beau, but it started me on the biggest mistake of my life; a totally misunderstood relationship with food, it having the upper hand, resulting into my warped thinking that if I keep losing weight and making the numbers on the scales my new God, then all in my life will be fine, nothing will ever go wrong again.

She became able to see that her unhealthy physical state was connected to her emotional pain and her unclear thinking.

education and practice in mindful eating, with a focus on awareness of emotional responses to food while eating.

For example, a common thought process might be, "I'm angry! What's wrong with me?" DBT helps to change this to, "I'm angry. I wonder why?" This ensures that anger and other "negative" emotions don't lead to shame and guilt. DBT is usually worked with a group, which can seem disturbing to people with eating disorders, but can be especially helpful.

Group therapy. Group therapy includes skill-teaching sessions that help people think about the connections between their feelings and actions. Group work also helps patients to practice new skills and behaviors and then report back about how they feel. Also, since a person with an eating disorder may feel a great deal of shame, when that person learns that she is not alone and that she can be in a relationship that is healthy, the shame lessens. In turn, there is less motivation for eating-disorder behaviors. Therapists note that eating-disorder recovery is more well-rounded with some form of group support involved to help relearn how to deal in relationships.

Group therapy can take place in a residential setting, in outpatient centers, or as part of work with a private therapist. There are a variety of group approaches. Therapy groups may be focused on the eating disorders themselves, or on issues that may be distracting a person from a healthy recovery. One advantage of this kind of therapy is that at least one professional therapist will manage the flow of the group.

Support groups provide safe environments for exploring recovery issues. Support groups have the advantage of being inexpensive (often free), and a well-run group offers a healthy community. But to be both effective and safe they need to be professionally run and connected to a clinical treatment program as needed.

Twelve-step groups, based on the successful model of Alcoholics Anonymous (AA), which include organizations such as Eating Disorders Anonymous (EDA), Eating Addictions Anonymous (EAA), Overeaters Anonymous (OA), and others, can help in establishing abstinence from eating-disorder behaviors through sharing and support from others who have been there. Groups are free.

Family therapy. The American Psychiatric Association notes that one hard part of many treatment plans is managing relationships with family and friends. These persons may not understand why the eating disorder is present, which will likely make the one with the disorder feel misunderstood. Many treatment programs have included education and help for loved ones, but now the family is often involved in specialized psychotherapy as well, both to give them support and to help them be part of the overall treatment plan.

A 2007 University of Chicago Medical Center study found that of patients in treatment for bulimia, almost 40 percent of those with family involvement were able to avoid bingeing and purging after six months, while only 18 percent of those with individual supportive psychotherapy could stop bingeing and purging at that time.

One family-therapy approach that seems effective is the Maudsley method, which ensures that no one is blamed for the eating disorder. It seeks to develop common goals for parents and their sons and daughters. (In the case of anorexia, for instance, the initial goal is weight gain). Some methods focus on the causes of eating disorders; the Maudsley method does not. Instead, it simply sees anorexia as a serious illness that needs immediate attention, and increasingly is being used for other eating disorders. The first phase of treatment helps the child to gain weight using a reward system managed by the parents. The second phase of treatment entails transferring control of eating back to the child. The child must demonstrate good weight gain to begin to assume responsibility for her own eating. The third phase begins when the child can maintain a weight of 95 percent of target weight without significant supervision from parents, and then can begin individual therapy to deal with underlying issues.

Nutritional counseling. Nutritionists work with other professionals whether treatment is inpatient or outpatient. The patient sees a nutritionist, sometimes weekly, sometimes less frequently (some people go for a one-time consultation), who will review a person's food intake, suggest things to add to balance nutrition and perhaps increase weight, and educate the person about how food affects the body in an effort to dispel any distorted thoughts they may have. The *psychonutritional* approach to the treatment of eating disorders is one in which psychotherapy and *medical nutrition therapy* carry through the entire recovery process.

Pharmacotherapy. Sometimes, medication is an important adjunct to psychotherapy, certainly if there is another illness like depression or OCD, and sometimes just to help manage symptoms better. The effectiveness of pharmaceutical treatment for eating disorders is still under study, but antidepressants or a *serotonin* reuptake inhibitor have been shown to have some effectiveness. Seroquel, or quetiapine, is a drug under investigation for use as a treatment for anorexia nervosa. Seroquel is approved for use in schizophrenia and has been used with some success in anorexia. Certain selective serotonin reuptake

inhibitors (SSRIs) have been shown to be helpful for weight maintenance and for resolving mood and anxiety symptoms associated with
anorexia. Evaluation and treatment may begin during hospitalization,
or during outpatient treatment with a psychotherapist.

Also, people with anorexia have symptoms in common with certain forms of depression. They both tend to have higher than normal
levels of cortisol, a brain hormone released in response to stress.
These connections may help to explain why those with eating disorders often suffer depression, and treatments for depression can help.

SPECIALIZED APPROACHES

Different eating disorders require slightly different treatment programs. Treatment of anorexia calls for a specific program that involves
three main phases: (1) restoring weight lost to severe dieting and
purging; (2) treating psychological disturbances such as distortion
of body image, low self-esteem, and interpersonal conflicts; and (3)
achieving long-term remission and rehabilitation, or full recovery.

Who Does What?

Which professional performs what function?

1. physician	a. prescribes psych medications
2. psychologist	b. leads therapy groups
3. social worker	c. tests body chemistry
4. psychiatrist	d. makes meal plans
5. nutritionist	e. evaluates metabolism
6. dietitian	f. formulates medications and supplements
7. pharmacist	g. determines and monitors physical condition
8. medical technician	h. guides emotional and mental treatments

(1:a&g); (2:b&h); (3:b&h); (4:a&g); (5:d&e); (6:d); (7:f); (8:c)

The primary goal of treatment for bulimia is to reduce or eliminate binge eating and purging behavior. Nutritional rehabilitation, psychosocial intervention, and medication management strategies are used to establish a pattern of regular, non-binge meals, improve attitudes related to the eating disorder, encourage healthy but not excessive exercise, and resolve co-occurring conditions such as mood or anxiety disorders. Individual psychotherapy (especially cognitive behavioral or interpersonal psychotherapy), group psychotherapy that uses a cognitive-behavioral approach, and family or marital therapy have been reported to be effective. The treatment goals and strategies for binge-eating disorder are similar to those for bulimia.

SIGNS OF PROGRESS

While recovery from any eating disorder is a long-term process, therapists from every school sense that a patient is ready to move on when, in addition to stabilizing body weight, he or she shows a shift in attitude toward a positive, long view of life, a breakdown of denial, a willingness to give up "fear foods" and other superstitions, and the ability to establish flexible, attainable goals that achieve success gradually and that aren't focused exclusively on food and body-issues.

Recovery can feel uncomfortable, as people are asked to give up patterns that have served as emotional protection. To help, therapists talk about "inoculation," warning them that they'll probably feel worse before they feel better. They may use a surgery analogy: "Immediately after surgery, you feel worse than before you went in, but in time, you feel better. Trying to change eating behaviors increases anxiety and stress. The anxiety will diminish with time." And treatment does take time. Some can find recovery in a year or less, but others need to stick with it for up to seven years, with ongoing follow-ups.

A young woman recovering from anorexia writes:

Overcoming my eating disorder was the hardest thing I've ever had to do. It was well worth the effort. I moved beyond getting better. I feel strong and proud of my accomplishment. I learned so much about myself and my family. I sought and received help from friends who were also suffering from eating disorders, and I helped my dad who was also suffering from depression. When I was going through therapy I felt as though I had wasted part of my life. Now I know that the years that I suffered made me who I am. They made me strong, and they gave me a purpose. I wouldn't go back and change a single day of my life, but I wouldn't spend another second starving myself, either.

DOES TREATMENT WORK?

Statistics vary on the success rates for treatment of eating disorders. Bulimia is somewhat easier to treat successfully than anorexia. For anorexia, success may be measured by the maintenance of 95 percent of normal weight for a specific length of time, but it's also something that a person may need to be aware of for the long term. Some studies indicate that as few as 50 percent of anorexia patients recover. ANRED (Anorexia Nervosa and Related Eating Disorders) reports that up to 20 percent of untreated anorectics die from the disorder. Of those who enter treatment, ANRED says that 60 percent recover completely. Another 20 percent make significant progress. Unfortunately, the last 20 percent remain chronic sufferers, even with treatment, and a few die even with treatment.

National Institutes of Health studies find that a combined approach to treatment is most effective. When the efforts of mental-health professionals are combined with those of other health professionals, the effects of treatment are most beneficial. Physicians treat any medical complications, and nutritionists advise on diet and eating regimens. The challenge of treating eating disorders is made more difficult by the metabolic changes associated with them, and nutritionists need to help patients maintain an appropriate calorie intake. Just to maintain a stable weight, individuals with anorexia may actually have to consume more calories than someone of similar weight and age without an eating disorder. For example, a nutritionist may be best able to determine caloric and nutrition needs, but a psychotherapist may be needed to help a patient become willing to take in the needed food.

BUILDING A PROFESSIONAL TREATMENT TEAM

Finding a combined approach is key. If you start treatment in a hospital or residential setting, a treatment team will be ready to go. But if you or your family seeks help on your own, you'll need to create a group of treatment professionals. What's the best approach? Get recommendations from others who have found successful treatment. Also, at the back of the book is a list of professional associations that can suggest reputable specialists in your area. For instance, the American Dietetic Association (http://www.eatright.org) provides a directory of qualified dietitians. Or, go to http://eatingdisorders.about.com for links. With guidelines like those, you can find an eating-disorder therapist in your area. Having a therapist you trust is important; it gives you the best chance to make good progress. Finding a dietitian who will provide

A Recovery Experience

Here's the experience of one obsessive exerciser and dieter:

I went to an eating-disorder recovery specialist. I had been to one before unsuccessfully, but this time the doctor had experience with cases like mine. I also went to a family practitioner with the request that he stay with me on this one—whether or not various therapies worked. Between these two doctors, I accepted a diagnosis of depression and an eating disorder. The recovery specialist suggested that perhaps the severity of the ups and downs I had been experiencing the past few years had been in some part chemical, and that maybe with drugs, I would not have to face such severity. Also, she offered me final relief from my exercise program. She was the first physician to say that maybe it was all right if I just didn't do it at all for awhile.

Recovery from all this was not instant, or even easy. It was scary to admit to myself the pain I was in, and very scary to relinquish control. But life was better even during recovery than it was inside the disorder. It took six months before I gained the first pound, and several more after that before life began to feel stable and normal. It took several attempts before I found the doctors who understood what was happening, and before a diagnosis became clear. The answers actually can be care, rest, and food—just the opposite of what I thought I had to put myself through.

care without judgment is another key to treatment. Find a physician who specializes in the treatment of eating disorders. Finally, you may want to find an eating-disorder support group in your area.

Whatever the setting for treatment, the longer you stick with it and the more consistent you are about it, the better the prospects for success. So it's important to find professionals with whom you are comfortable. Here are questions that ANRED suggests you or your family can ask a prospective counselor.

➤ What is your treatment approach?
➤ What can I expect to happen during sessions?

- ➤ How much experience have you had working with people who have eating disorders?
- ➤ What are your training, education, and licenses?
- ➤ How long do you think treatment will take?
- ➤ How often will we meet?
- ➤ If I think I need to, can I call you between sessions?
- ➤ What are your thoughts about using medications in the treatment of eating disorders?
- ➤ Could I be put in a hospital against my will? (This is a common fear. Get the facts at the beginning so you will know what to expect.)
- ➤ How much do sessions cost? Do you take insurance? What if my insurance will not cover all the costs of treatment?
- ➤ If I don't think I'm improving fast enough, I may feel like either you or I am failing. What can I do if that happens?

Whatever the treatment approach, the basic requirement for success is a combination of desire plus support. An individual's own willingness to get better strongly affects the outcome and is itself one of the "challenges" faced in any kind of treatment. In order to attempt changes in eating, people must have a strong desire to recover from the disorder. And because the efforts to make changes will increase their anxiety, and they will feel worse before feeling better, they will need ongoing support from those who care.

WHAT YOU NEED TO KNOW

- ➤ Treatment for eating disorders proceeds through a series of stages, beginning with assessment.
- ➤ Tested treatment techniques are practiced by a team of professionals.
- ➤ Treatment settings include hospitals, residential centers, and psychotherapists' offices.
- ➤ Success rates are good for people who stick with a combined approach to treatment and are ready to makes changes.

8

Managing Eating Disorders

The goal of treatment—inpatient, outpatient, group, individual—is to help people with eating disorders cope in a real world that surrounds them with food, diet ads, and bathroom scales. Many people with eating disorders observe that managing chemical dependency after treatment is easier than managing eating disorders. They point out that all an addict has to do is "not pick up the addictive substance," but someone with disordered eating still has to eat and exercise and look in the mirror and not let those activities become triggers.

Recovery from eating disorders can be a long-term and even lifelong process. It involves support and planning from family and friends as well as willingness to do the work required to move beyond the disorder. But treatment needn't go on indefinitely once symptoms have been relieved, as treatment gives patients tools for managing the issues themselves.

The goal of someone in recovery is usually simply to have a "normal" life, physically, mentally, and socially. To someone without an eating disorder, comments like this might just be met with, "So what?" But for someone who has lived through an eating disorder it's amazing.

I am overjoyed to report that I feel simply normal—happy and healthy. I live what I once assumed to be impossible and a farce—I eat when I am hungry, and I stop when I feel full. I exercise only to maintain my health—a few times a week at something I actually enjoy doing.

"The idea is to *not* have food be the center of my life," says a college student beginning recovery, "but to do that I have to be aware of how I eat!" A real balancing act.

How do you know if treatment is successful? That's a combination of eating non-"diet" meals, improvement of attitudes related to the eating disorder, encouragement of healthy but not excessive exercise, and resolution of conditions such as mood or anxiety disorders.

And it's more. Giving up an eating disorder is tough because the disorder can become a person's identity. "Who will I be without it?" is a very common and troubling question.

To get an idea of how much a part of life the eating disorder is, here are some comments written on the Something Fishy Web site supporting recovery.

▶ I am really afraid that I could really exceed beyond my wildest dreams. But I have never let myself try, because what if I succeed then fail miserably?

An Outline for "Normal"

National Institute of Mental Health research on interrupting the binge-eating cycle has shown that once a structured pattern of eating is established, the person experiences less hunger, less deprivation, and a reduction in negative feelings about food and eating. The two factors that increase the likelihood of bingeing—hunger and negative feelings—are reduced, which decreases the frequency of binges.

Counselors look for the following:

a. Three full meals/day

b. Adequate fluids

c. Covering all food groups? Types of food (desserts/fats) not eaten? Why? What's the fear/belief?

d. Patterns of restriction leading to bingeing

e. Are they depriving themselves of foods they love?

f. Do their meals have sufficient fat content to trigger satiety?

> I don't know what to do with my life and I cannot cope without direction.
> I need help believing in myself.
> I don't know who I am or what I'm all about.
> I have no confidence in myself or my abilities.
> I am starting to become comfortable with the idea that I am ordinary and that there's nothing wrong with that.
> I hold back from full recovery because I hang on to anorexia as an excuse to not chase after my real goals.

The professionals at ANRED describe recovery as "much more than the abandonment of starving and stuffing." At minimum it includes the physical results of the maintenance of normal or near-normal weight, and in women, regular menstrual periods. In terms of food, a person in recovery eats a varied diet of normal foods (not just low-cal, nonfat, nonsugar items) and has eliminated or greatly reduced irrational food fears. Socially, he or she can engage in age-appropriate relationships with family members and one or more mutually satisfying friendships with healthy, normal people. Such relationships involve mutual give-and-take and a minimum of caretaking and "parenting" behavior. As appropriate, people in recovery may participate in romantic relationships with people who are accepting of all aspects of themselves. They're able to engage in fun activities that have nothing to do with food, weight, or appearance.

As individuals, people in recovery from eating disorders have a strong repertoire of problem-solving skills. They understand the process of choices and consequences, realizing that they don't have to be "perfect." They have an awareness of cultural demands for unrealistic thinness, and they can employ effective ways of repudiating those demands and protecting themselves from them. In short, they have a good sense of themselves, and have developed individualized goals and plans.

MEETING DAILY CHALLENGES

Managing an eating disorder is an ongoing project. This doesn't mean that someone has to struggle with the disorder forever. He will need to be aware of it, and over time its pull may weaken.

The way that people manage their eating disorders over the long term is to deal with them on a daily basis. They practice taking the focus off weight: People in recovery from eating disorders are encouraged not to weigh themselves regularly. (In fact, frequent—daily or more—weighing can be seen as a sign of an active eating disorder.) A focus on weight as an absolute number triggers a drive to diet. Each person has his or her own healthy weight.

They also need to still maintain enough focus on food that in the long term they develop patterns of healthy eating, designed for their unique bodies. Defined from a psychological standpoint, healthy eating must be based on freedom and flexibility. In recovery, healthy eating means eating over the whole range of foods and choosing freely, not rigidly about what's "safe."

All of this may sound like simple common sense to someone without an eating disorder, but those who are breaking free from these illnesses find it useful to employ behavior tools daily to develop and maintain balanced eating patterns.

Those with anorexia need to get help with designing a meal plan that provides all the nutrition their bodies need for health and growth. Thirty to 60 minutes of exercise or physical activity three to five days a week is healthy; more than may be too much if you have an eating disorder. Check with your physician to approve your meal plans and exercise schedule before you begin. Ask your physician and a responsible adult you trust for an honest, objective opinion of your weight. Let them keep an eye on you, and if they say you are "normal" or too thin, believe them. When the old fears return and you start to "feel fat," ask yourself what you are really afraid of. Then take steps to deal with the threat if it is real, or dismiss it if it is not real.

Those with bulimia and binge-eating disorder can benefit by following a healthy meal plan, one that manages weight and reduces risks of medical problems. This meal plan should meet nutritional needs and be flexible enough to include reasonable amounts of fun foods.

HALT is an acronym used by addiction-recovery specialists to remind those in recovery not to let themselves get too *H*ungry, too *A*ngry, too *L*onely, or too *T*ired, as these feelings can trigger relapse. These tips are just as helpful for those in recovery from eating disorders. Don't let yourself get pulled in too many directions by too many people, too many demands, and too many responsibilities. All these states are powerful binge triggers. Watch for them, and when they first appear, deal with them in a healthy manner instead of letting the tension build until bingeing and purging become the only release you can imagine. Instead of getting bored or overwhelmed, try to stay in balance: Stay comfortably busy and avoid unstructured time, which can lead to binge temptations. Make sure you get enough sleep; at least seven hours every night.

Keep in touch! Make sure that you spend time with friends and loved ones—in person is best; phone and e-mail can substitute, but only once in a while. Enjoy being with people you love and those who love you. Every day do something fun, something relaxing, something energizing. All of these simple-sounding activities can keep you emotionally "full" and reduce the need to fill yourself with food.

Take control of your life. Make choices thoughtfully and deliberately. Make your living situation comfortable. Make yourself comfortable, too, by monitoring your "self-talk." When you find yourself falling into negative thoughts about yourself, your appearance, your abilities, and your accomplishments, switch to a positive inventory.

Keep in touch with yourself. It may have taken some time and effort to become aware of your feelings and not use food to hide from them, so try to keep tabs on how you feel. When you're "off," get in touch with a friend or turn to a favorite activity.

LIFE WITH AN EATING DISORDER

Is long-term recovery possible? Yes, eating disorders are treatable, reports the *International Journal of Eating Disorders*. The folks who do best work with physicians and counselors who help them resolve both the medical and psychological issues that contribute to, or result from, disordered eating. In other words, a healthy relationship with food is about more than eating habits.

People in recovery from eating disorders also find some surprising challenges—and rewards—that have nothing to do with food. For instance, they say that learning to communicate can be the hardest part of the process. And not just learning to express emotions, but to feel them at all. But they also discover that the very emotions they were hiding from through food behaviors become some of the greatest adventures of their lives.

As one of those in recovery from eating disorders explains, "One of the things we will need to learn to do is to find better ways to cope with emotions. We have learned that our behaviors were good 'emotion blockers.' It is easier to think about eating, not eating, eating too much, how many calories we just had or will avoid . . . than it is to deal with our feelings and emotions."

It was once thought that family conflicts and inadequacies set eating disorders in motion. Now it appears that the media contribute as well. For instance, all those diet-pill ads, "six-pack abs" promotions and the like. Every week there seems to be a new breakthrough diet, and every week at least a few of the books on the bestseller lists are related to diet, while some of the most popular channels on TV are about food and cooking. It would seem that not just eating gets disordered, but the emphasis on weight, looks, and meals can be confusing.

Big changes. There's no such thing as a "small change" in managing eating disorders. For just as treatment for eating disorders involves a lot more than regulating food intake, so learning to live without the eating disorder requires changes that are deeper than many realize. Eating disorders are not just "bad habits." The feelings run deep. When young people are able to explain what it feels like to have an eating disorder, and to break free from it, the power of the disorders becomes clear.

"Sometimes the weight of my sadness is bone-crushing, like the pressure of water down deep," is how one girl describes her disorders. Another explanation for hanging on to a destructive pattern: "The ED was the only constant in my life, the only thing which felt unchanging regardless of what external events happened. The ED was the only guarantee, the only certainty, the only thing loyal to me throughout everything that came my way."

Given the kinds of struggles people experience with eating disorders, it seems logical to want to get better. Some girls describe why that's not so easy: "I felt too ashamed, too dirty, too embarrassed, and too scared to tell you that I couldn't cope without hurting myself." Another teen says, "I desperately want to be accepted," and she felt being "thin" was the only way she could do that. Another puts it more vividly: "Sometimes I feel like I don't belong anywhere and I feel like an alien and that I don't belong in this time because my outlook feels so foreign."

One girl who is almost ready to let go of it says, "I don't like the eating disorder; I just am having a hard time disliking it." Another is nervous about recovery because although she is scared that the disorder will kill her, she is also afraid of not winning the battle of recovery.

Realistic expectations. Given all the challenges that daily management of eating disorders brings, it's not surprising that there are setbacks. Relapses happen: Someone binges briefly, or goes back into diet mode. Relapses can frighten the person with the disorder and those around them. So keep in mind that these "lapses" can be expected and can educate. All that's needed is to review the positive skills learned and practice them again.

ANRED has a lot of suggestions for relapse prevention. Another way to view this advice is that these are suggestions simply for living well. To someone without an eating disorder, it seems like simple common sense. For instance:

If you have anorexia nervosa, ANRED recommends eating a variety of foods. When you start to get overwhelmed by "feeling fat," they advise, "Instead of dwelling on your appearance, think it through and count all the good things in your life." To "accept that your body shape is determined in part by genetics" sounds simple enough, but acceptance can be tough.

Or, for those who have struggled with bulimia, ANRED's suggestion is, "Never let yourself get so hungry that the urge to binge is overwhelming. Instead, eat regularly. And select food that tastes good." They also advise, "Take charge of your life. And make choices about your work and your friends." They remind people with bulimia: "If you feel yourself slipping back into unhealthy habits, call your therapist and

Which Goals Work?

Which goals are healthy ones for someone with an eating disorder?

1. Wearing a size seven.

2. Winning a marathon.

3. Balancing work and fun.

4. Eating only protein.

5. Setting one's own career goals.

6. Learning to say no/yes.

Unhealthy goals:

1. Size does *not* matter.

2. Probably not healthy—unless it's part of a life plan and not an obsession.

4. On the contrary; experts say that "rainbow" eating, of a full range of foods, is a healthy goal.

Healthy goals:

3. Balance takes effort, but it's worth it!

5. Planning life and making one's own choices is important.

6. Making decisions rather than reacting to compulsions is a new, healthy mode.

schedule an appointment. Returning to counseling in no way means you have failed. It means only that it's time to reevaluate and fine-tune your recovery plan."

INFORMATION FOR PARENTS AND LOVED ONES

It isn't just those with the ED who have to struggle. If you're living with someone who has an eating disorder, you face demands before treatment, during treatment, and after treatment. You need special guidance, too. Watching someone you love grapple with an eating disorder can be disturbing. It need not be paralyzing as well. Find out what to say and what not to say, and when and how you can step into the situation with strength and compassion.

Here's what it feels like to live with someone with an eating disorder:

> My older sister is severely bulimic. I don't want her to die, but, at the same time, I am frustrated because my life has been so painfully disrupted by her disease. I feel like I'm *her* older sister or even her mother. I feel guilty about being angry that she is sick, but at the same time it is so emotionally, spiritually, and mentally draining to live with her and to love her.

What is it like to be an eating disorder caregiver? Those with eating disorders need help, and family and friends often step in to be eating disorder caregivers. The impact on these persons can be life-changing.

There is only so much you can do to help someone with an eating disorder. We can point the way but we can't force recovery. And the pain of trying to live someone else's life can destroy the helper's life, as well. So it's vital for many reasons to find help for yourself.

There's support available for you, too, as a friend or relative of someone who has an eating disorder. Try the same Web sites and electronic bulletin boards suggested in the appendix for a start.

How eating disorders hurt caregivers' relationships. ANRED notes that it is easy to become isolated when you are a caregiver for a person with an eating disorder. It strains the caregiver's relationship with family and friends, as well as the relationship with the person who has the eating disorder.

It's also very important for anyone caring for someone with an eating disorder to receive support, too. They are reminded to nourish themselves physically, emotionally, and spiritually. Every day they should spend time, in person or by phone or e-mail, with their own friends, and doing things they can take pride in—to have something to look forward to every day, something that's fun and pleasurable.

Caregivers are reminded that they need support for themselves. Family therapy can be of great help—even if it doesn't get the eating disorder sufferer into treatment. The treatment team can point caregivers to mutual support groups, as well as formal therapy.

GROUP HELP

The best and most important aspect of treatment of an eating disorder is talking about it. Next in importance can be hearing how other people deal with it. Support groups offer the kind of shared experience that can get you through the tough times, whether you have an eating disorder or live with someone who does.

NEDA offers some suggestions for getting the most from support groups. A support group can provide valuable encouragement and a safe place to problem solve and talk about challenges. But NEDA suggests being wary of informal groups led by parents or people who themselves are still recovering from an eating disorder. The most effective therapy groups are led or supervised by a professional mental-health therapist as part of an integrated treatment program. Also, if a lay leader is not confirmed in his or her own recovery, there may be temptation to relapse if group dynamics become intense and the focus remains on food and weight behaviors instead of on problem-solving.

In addition to therapy groups, mutual self-help groups can provide support. Some of these, like Overeaters Anonymous, are in the 12-step model. Others might be groups centered in churches or hospitals.

A member of Overeaters Anonymous recounts her experiences:

I would go to Weight Watchers and lose some weight, and then go out of control. I gained 100 pounds in a few years, which I lost and gained again in increments as the years went on. This crazy cycle of controlled eating and then bingeing ran my life for over 20 years.

One day I met a woman who said she had lost 50 pounds by going to Overeaters Anonymous (OA). So 11 years ago, I went there to lose weight, and instead I gained a new way of living life. At first I was pretty turned off about OA. I thought that the people at the meeting were "too sick" for me; I just had a problem with food—it took me quite a while to understand just how deep the disease ran. When I hit bottom and realized that I was powerless over my food and weight compulsion and that my life was unmanageable, I began to work the 12-step program of recovery in OA.

The OA program has given me my life back, and helped me to let go of the weight without dieting. For me, the hardest thing to get over are the residual body-image issues that still bother me, but it's nowhere near how it used to be. Long gone are the days of eating from Thursday night straight through to Sunday night. I have hope now, and I take things one day at a time, and sometimes, one meal at a time. I have learned that if you are willing to go to any lengths, you can recover.

One thing that family and friends can learn from the treatment they get themselves is how futile and even self-defeating it is to do too much for someone who has an eating disorder. This kind of "enabling" can make the situation a great deal worse. What it boils down to is that someone with an eating disorder can manage her new patterns—but no one else can manage her life.

WHAT YOU NEED TO KNOW

▶ The long-term goals of recovery are balance in eating and activities.
▶ People manage their recovery by planning and using daily tools.
▶ Food issues and emotional issues are so tightly tied together that managing one requires managing the other.
▶ People who are close to people with eating disorders can find much-needed help for themselves, too.

9

Helping a Friend

If just telling someone to eat better would "fix" an eating disorder, no one would be trapped in the cycles of anorexia or bulimia. Those and other disorders can be so painful to watch in people that we care about that the urge to help is strong, but helping is not always easy. So what can you do for a friend or family member who is living with an eating disorder? Before they seek treatment, you can help them find help. During treatment, you can be supportive and learn as much as you can. For the long-term after treatment, you can help them enjoy their lives. Plus, you can work to help yourself.

HELPING BEFORE TREATMENT

The first step for a helper, as for someone in need of help, is awareness. Keep in mind that people around those with disorders can live in denial, too.

If you are worried about your friend's eating behaviors or attitudes, it is important to express your concerns in a loving and supportive way. It is also necessary to discuss your worries early on, rather than waiting until your friend has endured many of the damaging physical and emotional effects of eating disorders.

If you suspect that someone you know has an eating disorder and want to help, look for clues: laxative wrappers or diuretic packages found in the trash can be used to confront him or her with reality.

Writing in About.com, eating-disorder expert Kelly A. Boy, R.N., CPNP, offers clues to determining if someone you care about has an eating disorder.

Does it seem that your friend has an obsession with weight and food? It might seem like your friend talks about food and nothing else, and not just from occasional enthusiasm about things she enjoys, but about exactly how many calories and fat grams are in everything that she—or you or anyone else—is eating, or thinking about eating. Yet despite this constant attention to food, your friend avoids hanging out with you and other friends during meals. For example, he or she avoids the school cafeteria at lunch or the restaurant where you usually meet on weekends. When you do spend any mealtime with your friend, he or she lets you know about a new dramatic or very restrictive diet. You may notice that he or she cuts food into tiny pieces, moves food around on the plate instead of eating it, and is very precise about how food is arranged on the plate.

Or, your friend seems to feel the need to exercise all the time, even when sick or exhausted. There's no such thing as a fun hike or just hanging around the gym—he's intense about a rigid exercise routine. (Remember that obsessive exercise is also a kind of eating disorder.)

Does it seem that, despite losing a lot of weight, your friend always talks about how fat he or she is? Poor body image can be a sign of anorexia. On the other hand, does your friend appear to be gaining a lot of weight even though you never see him or her eat? Compulsive eaters usually eat in private.

Maybe your friend goes to the bathroom a lot, especially right after meals, or maybe you've heard your friend vomiting after eating. Your friend frequently takes laxatives. These may be signs of purging.

Your friend starts to wear big or baggy clothes, and it's not part of the fashion trend in your circle. People with eating disorders often wear baggy clothes to conceal a body he or she doesn't like, or one they're keeping secret. A compulsive eater may be overweight—but someone with anorexia may want to hide the fact that she's growing pathologically thin.

Finally, you may notice that your friend has a tendency to faint, bruises easily, is very pale, or starts complaining of being cold more than usual. These can all be symptoms of a variety of health problems (all of which should be medically checked), but they are all often signs of underweight or poor nutrition.

If your friend has these symptoms and you're concerned, the first thing to do might be to talk to your friend, privately, about what you have noticed. Tell your friend that you're worried. Be as gentle as possible, and try to really listen to and be supportive of your friend and what he or she is going through.

It's normal for a person with an eating disorder to be defensive and angry when confronted for the first time. Try not to get angry back at your friend; just remind him or her that you care. Trying to help someone who doesn't think he or she needs help can be hard; people with eating disorders often have trouble admitting, even to themselves, that they have a problem. Of course, it's not your job to diagnose your friend; that's the job of a doctor.

What to do. Being a supportive friend also means learning how to behave around someone with an eating disorder. It's important to avoid talking about food, or being overly watchful of your friend's eating habits, food amounts, and choices. This can make someone just retreat further into isolation.

Remember how seriously people with eating disorders take their situation, and try not to sound judgmental with comments like, "If you'd just eat or stop exercising, you'll get better." Your friend probably knows full well that this is true, but is just not able to do it. Your friend needs support more than criticism. So it's important, too, to avoid reinforcing the idea that this is all about your friend's physical appearance, but rather make clear that this is about his or her safety and happiness. Most importantly, remind your friend that you care, no matter how he or she looks.

The Indirect Approach

Think about ways to approach a difficult topic in a way that doesn't scare your friend away. You might want to talk about "someone else" who seems to be losing a lot of weight or showing other signs of an ED, and say something like, "It makes me think of what I saw on TV about eating disorders. I sure hope she finds a way to get help." Or observe something like, "It must be really painful to have to keep secrets like those people do." Try to let your friend know that you're aware of the problem and are open to being helpful without judging.

If you feel comfortable with a direct approach, here's how it might go:

1. Choose a time when you can be calm. Getting upset doesn't help.
2. Present your concerns in a gentle but firm manner: For instance, "I've noticed that your eating (or exercising) is getting out of whack, and your weight is scary. Can I help?"
3. Recommend that she get treatment, and offer specific resources. "I've read that eating problems can be really unhealthy, and there's a place right here where they can help."
4. Be persistent: "I'm sure I'm driving you nuts, but did you check out that Web site?"
5. Be concrete. For instance, set a time by which you want the person to get outside help.

What not to do. Remember that eating disorders are not just about appearance or superficial behavior. They run deep, so experts suggest some approaches to avoid.

1. **Don't** comment on her appearance; it's not really about looks!
2. **Don't** discuss specifics about nutrition. Someone with an eating disorder probably knows more than enough, but knowledge doesn't mean change.
3. **Don't** demand that your friend eat differently. If he could, he would.
4. **Don't** try to shame your friend into different behavior. Your friend is likely to be ashamed already.
5. **Don't** be put off by attempts to make you think you're foolish for wanting to help. Making fun of you could be part of your friend's irrational protection of his or her disorder.
6. **Don't** keep your friend's eating behavior a secret for her—even if you've said you would. The best thing you can do is to tell someone who can help, like a responsible adult. Revealing the secret might lose a friendship, but not revealing it can lose the friend herself.

If your concerns increase and your friend still seems to be in denial, talk to your parents, the school guidance counselor or nurse, or your friend's parents. This isn't easy to do because it can feel like

Keep It in the "I"

Another way to keep your friend from getting too defensive is to try to focus on your own concerns, and use "I" statements, rather than "you" statements. Instead of statements like "You have an eating disorder" or "You're obsessed with food," Try "I'm worried that you have lost so much weight so quickly." It's also a good idea to explain specific things your friend has said or done that have made you worry. Pick some items from the list of clues above. Then say you hope your friend would check with a doctor.

betraying a friend, but it's often necessary to get your friend the help he or she needs.

So instead of pushing at your friend with cranky questions such as, "You look awful; are you sick?" remember that the person who has an eating disorder may already have low self-esteem. Being critical or angrily apprehensive will only make her feel worse—and may drive her away from you.

It's better to approach a close friend or someone in your family with a caring statement, such as, "You've lost a lot of weight recently and I'm concerned about you," followed by, "I'm here for you when you want to talk." Anything you can say to communicate your affection and concern is more beneficial than a threatening, "Would you just eat?" or "Stay out of the damn bathroom!"

Knowing your limitations is key. You are not the person who will end the eating disorder; leave that to a qualified group of professionals. But you can increase the odds that the person you love will make the choices needed to recover.

HELPING DURING TREATMENT

Families and friends offering eating-disorder recovery support and encouragement can play an important role in the success of the treatment program. The National Institute of Mental Health observes that treatment can save the life of someone with an eating disorder. Friends, relatives, teachers, and physicians all play an important role in helping the ill person start and stay with a treatment program. Encouragement, caring, and persistence, as well as information about eating disorders and their dangers, may be needed to convince the ill person to get help, stick with the treatment, or try again. Participating in the family programs that are available is a key way to support recovery.

Remember that the longer people stick with treatment the better their chance of success. Remember too that separation from the disordered patterns can be really hard, so people often want to quit. The

How It Feels

Helping is more effective when we offer help that someone wants, rather than the help we think they should have. Here are some expressions, shared on the Something Fishy Web site, of what people with eating disorders want from their helpers and supporters:

▸ "Sometimes I just want you to listen, not talk, not interrupt, not offer advice or suggestions. Sometimes all I want is you to sit there and listen and to feel like I have been heard."

▸ "Words and actions hurt me even though they weren't meant to."

▸ "I cry when you hug me because of the emptiness and pain I know I'll feel when you finally do let me go."

▸ "I sometimes need your help, but I'm not sure how to tell you this."

▸ "I cry when no one is around."

▸ "I am unable to see my potential right now, but it helps me to hear you when you tell me it's there."

▸ "What I want most is to just hear that I am okay just the way I am, even if my natural state isn't common, normal, or cool."

▸ "I don't want you to give up on me."

It's as important to listen to what they have to say as to focus on telling them what you want them to hear.

most important support you can offer is a firm refusal to let them talk you into letting them quit.

Do your best to focus on the positive: For instance, praise your friend for doing well, rather than express regret about the past or fear about the future. Your upbeat attitude can help her want to get better—and she has to do the work if treatment is to succeed. Here are one young woman's observations about treatment:

> There is no magic answer. What worked for me might not work for you. You have to find the way that's best for you. But one thing I can say is that I truly believe that you can only have recovery if you want it more than anything else in the entire world. You have to be "sick" of being "sick" and be willing to do whatever it takes to get better. For me, that was six weeks in the hospital, following a rigid food plan designed by a nutritionist, outpatient therapy, support groups, and reading books.
>
> What didn't work was spending time with negative people who seemed to thrive on being sick. Once I started surrounding myself with healthy, happy people, I started to feel healthier and happier myself. The positive-thinking stuff really works. Of course, I didn't believe what I was telling myself at first, but eventually, what I told myself became reality.

Stay in touch with your friend and focus on the positive. ANRED notes that it's good to admit that you aren't going to make your friend better through your own efforts. It will take time, persistence, and a lot of help from trained clinicians. The goal is to continue to point out the advantages of getting that help. Your consistent care can ease her fears of change and encourage her to embrace the possibility that there's something better waiting for her.

HELPING FOR THE LONG TERM

Once families were blamed for eating disorders. This attitude has changed, but there are some family problems that contribute to disordered eating patterns. Chaotic and disorganized families, "perfect" rigid families, those where parents are battling, or those where children are asked to take on adult roles are examples. For successful recovery from eating disorders, families need support as well: Treatment centers and individual eating-disorder therapists often include a family component in the normal course of treatment. This will often begin after the child is physically stabilized. It is common to work to uncover roles, communication styles, and areas of control or neglect.

People still may look at the family of someone with an eating disorder and come to a quick conclusion about how the disorder came to be. This can make coping as a family even more difficult, so that makes it even more important to participate in family counseling. Even if your loved one does not want treatment, she or he will see firsthand that counseling can offer a healthy approach to problem-solving. It will also help you to avoid turning to negative behaviors yourself—like drinking or overmedicating—as a way to deal with family stress.

Counselors say that one of the most important things you can do to support the long-term recovery of a loved one is to be a model yourself of healthy eating and exercise. So if you cook and eat healthy foods, and talk about the difference between dieting and meal planning, you can offer a concrete example of health. In your conversations, be careful not to overly criticize your own or anyone else's body. Praise (or criticism) for what a person does rather than for how he looks sends an important message about what really matters.

Getting involved in activities like hiking, biking, sports, or swimming, and trying to involve the whole family, is much healthier—and more fun—than focusing on intense "fitness." The same applies to food; meals should be satisfying emotionally as well as physically, so don't engage in power struggles over food. Do the best you can to provide healthy eating opportunities, but leave the rest to a therapist—yours or the disordered eater's.

Don't arrange your life—or your meal schedule—around the needs of the family member with an eating disorder. Her need for control may be huge, but she needs to learn that she must control only her own life.

If you are close to someone who has an eating disorder, you need to be just as aware as this person is that the disorder is a genuine health issue, not a statement about someone's character, lack of "will," or moral fitness. But even people who can see and identify an eating disorder are often at a loss about what to do or how to help, and their frustration can lead to anger. It's all too easy to assume that the disordered behavior is willful, rather than compulsive, and that anger, punishment, or control will "fix" it. "She hurt me so much. I can't sleep at night worrying about how she is doing and how long she will live. Why is she doing this to me?" While such feelings among family and friends are understandable, they only worsen the problems engendered by an eating disorder.

It might help to keep in mind that the person with the eating disorder is in pain, too. As one describes it:

> I know what it's like to think constantly about food. I know the joy and the agony of stepping on the scale many times a day. I know the

guilt of eating, the pressure to exercise. I know the triumph of not eating and of exercising more than anyone else. I know how alone it can feel. I know the horror of eating and not being able to stop. I know the hundred little distortions that helped me hide my eating disorder from me and others.

On the other hand, watching someone slowly starve, or wear himself down with overexercise, or eat herself sick by gorging and purging, can be excruciating. It's almost as painful to witness these eating disorders as it is to experience them in person. However, these disorders can be so powerful that professional attention is necessary.

So take care of yourself. Remember that you are under stress. One of you is already in pain due to the eating disorder—it is not helpful to make your life miserable, too. If you are a friend, spend only as much time with your friend as you can manage and let her know what your limits are. If you are family, make sure you find relief in activities you really enjoy, and turn to counseling to keep your own mind and emotions clear about this very painful situation—a situation that you did *not* cause, and you can't cure.

PREVENTING RELAPSE

Lapses or more serious relapses are common—almost to be expected—in recovery from eating disorders. They can be caused by the smallest trigger: anything from stress from school or family, to coping with something that a friend is going through. Part of counseling is to help

How It Feels to Live with Someone with an Eating Disorder

"My 22-year-old sister has bulimia. My parents asked me to move in with her this year to 'keep an eye' on her, but to be honest, after almost five months of it I can't handle it any more. I try to be understanding and I know she has problems, but in some ways I just feel so angry at her. I'm only 20 and I'm trying to find my own way in the world and I can't take this responsibility."

the person with an eating disorder to be aware of them and avoid them. If you live with someone in recovery, you can also be aware of possible relapse triggers.

These can include any high-pressure situations, like midterms and finals at school, or any major exams that are in the near future, as well as a competition in a sport coming up. Interpersonal stress can be difficult, too, as when someone is feeling increasing pressure from family (especially parents). The loss of a friend or family member through a move, divorce, death, or leaving for college, can be stressful. Going through a painful breakup with a girlfriend or boyfriend, or being rejected, can obviously be tough, but so can having a friend that is going through a rough time. Fear of recovery itself can be a trigger, but so can being around those that are engrossed with their own eating disorders while one is trying to recover.

A person in recovery may also have inner triggers to relapse. Even though she is working on balanced eating, she's learned she may be on the way back to unhealthy patterns when she starts feeling not just a need to escape from stress and problems, but also an increasing need to be in control of many things, or when her perfectionist thinking returns or becomes stronger. The beginnings of a new way of life can be exciting and hopeful, but when it begins to become a daily routine, sometimes there's a letdown. Feelings of hopelessness or growing sadness can stir up old beliefs that only being thin brings happiness and only a "diet" brings control.

Her behavior may then begin to slip, and she finds herself looking in mirrors and weighing herself more often, or skipping meals—while being dishonest about engaging in those behaviors. Then come the old patterns that recovery was breaking her of, including get-togethers that involve food, feeling the need to isolate, even thoughts of suicide.

Those close to such people may need to be sensitive to clues to that old behavior—but also need to remember that it is their loved one who must manage the relapse urges.

In treatment, patients are urged to be aware of dangers and think through their actions. Family and friends can learn from counselors how to remind the recovering person to work through the urge to relapse.

For instance, sometimes what helps prevent people from relapsing is having them make a list of things they can do instead of starving or purging. Things like cleaning, playing with a pet, going on the computer, talking with a friend, going camping, listening to a favorite CD, and so on can help.

On a more positive note. It's not all about "preventing relapse." It's also about enjoying life! Once your friend or relative is in recovery, your focus needs to be even less on "their problem."

People with eating disorders say that the best help is acceptance— not to comment on appearance or eating habits, but just to live life, as they would like to. So try to forget about food as a focus and remember why you became this person's friend, until it becomes time to enjoy life together again.

WHAT YOU NEED TO KNOW

> ‣ Family and friends can help someone with an eating disorder before, during, and after treatment.
> ‣ Others need to remember that they may need their own kinds of support to help themselves.
> ‣ Relapses are common, but can be avoided or lessened in intensity.

10 ║|║

Paying for Care

Obtaining insurance coverage for the optimal treatment of eating disorders can be challenging. Treatment providers make their treatment recommendations, insurance companies decide what they will support financially, and it is not unusual for there to be significant differences of opinion in the appropriate level of care. Trying to figure out and manage the payment for treatment can add to the confusion of how to best get help for a serious illness.

According to a national survey by the National Eating Disorders Association (NEDA), 96 percent of Americans believe eating disorders are serious illnesses; 81 percent believe eating disorders can be successfully treated; and 76 percent believe that eating disorders should be covered by insurance companies just like any other illness. In part because of this widening awareness of these disorders, more people are seeking treatment for eating disorders than ever before, and treatment centers are expanding around the country. A significant number of patients may not get their care covered 100 percent by insurance, and may need to pay for it themselves.

FACTS ABOUT COVERAGE

As few as one in 10 people with eating disorders receive appropriate treatment, according to data gathered by the South Carolina Department of Mental Health. About 80 percent of the girls and women who have accessed care for their eating disorders do not get the intensity of treatment they need to stay in recovery—they are often sent home weeks earlier than the recommended stay. This is in part because of the cost.

What it costs. Treatment of an eating disorder in the United States can range from $500 per day to $2,000 per day. The average cost for a month of inpatient treatment is $30,000. It is estimated that individuals with eating disorders may need anywhere from a week to six months of inpatient care. The cost of outpatient treatment, including therapy and medical monitoring, can extend to $100,000 or more.

Who is covered. Insurance policies' coverage varies from state to state, company to company, and even according to the individual contracts an insurer may have with an employer or with the insured. For individuals or families with no insurance, public funding—from Medicaid, Medicare, or the State Children's Health Insurance Program (SCHIP)—may be available for young people.

It may be that, as eating disorder treatment becomes more mainstream, coverage will expand. Legislative efforts continue to expand coverage for mental illnesses. A recently passed "mental health parity bill" moved that effort closer to reality, but until there's a nationwide policy, people must work within the state-by-state rules for public and private funding for treatment.

Families do have choices, including picking treatment formats that fit within the coverage available. Understanding how the system works can improve their chances of obtaining payment for services. It may be possible to have treatment paid for, so parents should try not to get discouraged.

Limitations and how to work with them. NEDA, like other advocacy groups for people with ED, suggests a plan for getting payment for treatment, whether from private insurance or community agencies. NEDA suggests anyone seeking insurance payment for eating disorders be prepared with the following information:

1. Eating-disorder diagnosis
2. Other psychiatric diagnoses
3. Physiological complications of the eating disorder
4. Level of care recommended (outpatient, inpatient, partial hospital, residential, or intensive outpatient)
5. Anticipated duration of recommended treatment
6. Professionals needed and their required expertise

Families: If you have insurance, first study your policy to determine if there are mental-health benefits and if they include an amount for inpatient or residential treatment and an amount for outpatient treatment. Most policies also include major medical benefits, which may be easier to tap than the mental-health benefits. Ask your employer or call the company if it's not clear. (Note that you may not have to give your name or details or your case to ask basic coverage questions, although many companies will require this information.) By 2010, insurance companies will be required to provide mental health benefits on the same level as medical benefits, as a result of the passage of the Mental Health Parity Act of 2008.

Am I insured? What are my health insurance benefits? What are the deductibles, co-pays, and annual and lifetime limits of my insurance benefits? Often health insurance has limits on what type of treatment services it will reimburse; usually there will be a limit on how many days and how many times in the course of a year it will pay for treatment. Typically, insurance pays for a limited number of outpatient sessions (generally 30) and a limited set of inpatient hospital or residential treatment days per year. Many insurers also impose lifetime limits on the amount of care covered by the policy and caps on the number of times you can be treated for what they consider nonmedical conditions.

Many insurers employ "utilization reviewers" to make decisions about what treatment they will pay for. Utilization reviewers then inform the hospital, treatment program, family, patient, or provider of what they will cover and what they will pay for. This management of continuing care often means that the treatment program must get permission every 10 sessions or, for inpatients, every one to three days, to continue payment for treatment services. If treatment providers do not cooperate, reimbursement may be stopped. If approval for payment is stopped, the patient and providers need to determine if it is safe to discharge the patient. If not, the patient may need to remain in the hospital. An appeal may be done or, in some cases, arrangements made for self or private pay.

What are the criteria the health insurance company will use to decide if it will allow admission to treatment and will pay for the treatment? Often when you call the insurance company's toll-free number to get authorization for treatment services, there will be a utilization reviewer at the other end. The utilization reviewer uses what is called "medical necessity criteria" to decide whether and in which in-network settings (inpatient, residential, outpatient) the insurer may pay for treatment services. However, authorization may be given after a professional assessment. Individual insurance companies have their own medical-necessity criteria, and these can vary from company to company. If your insurance does not think these criteria are met, you may be denied payment for treatment services. Authorization for in-patient care can be difficult.

Whatever benefits you have, there is likely a specific list of practitioners the company will accept, so the next step would be to match providers in your area with those approved by the company.

IF INSURANCE AND TREATMENT DON'T MATCH

Obtaining payment for appropriate care can be difficult and complicated. Insurance policies often have annual and lifetime limits on payment for care. One option is to ask the individual company if, for example, payment for refeeding for anorexia on a medical floor is considered a "medical benefit" rather than a "mental-health benefit."

It is not unusual for utilization reviewers to issue what they call a "denial"—in essence, they do not authorize payment for care. If your treatment provider believes that the case is "appropriate" and they can "justify" (utilization-review terms) to the insurance company that the case meets the company's medical-necessity criteria, the denial may be overturned. Interestingly, some states publish the percentages of denials overturned on appeal for each insurance company that does business in their state. Also, there are several levels of appeal within each company, and most states have an insurance commission that will do a final appeal review.

Filling the gap. Find out if you are eligible for Medicaid or Medicare and whether the treatment program you're interested in accepts those forms of payment. To find help with insurance issues, parents should go to their employer's human-resources department, the business office of the treatment program you are interested in, or your state insurance commission.

Often a private health insurer or Medicaid will identify someone, frequently a nurse-practitioner, to coordinate or "manage" the care provided. It is very important to know who that person is and to communicate with her directly. Care managers also may be used to track whether a patient is moving through levels of care.

Finally, you can turn to your local social-service agency, where a caseworker or advocate can help unravel the rules.

Get Help!

In case of acute need for medical care, go to the emergency room.

People also are reluctant to seek help because they want to keep the eating disorder private. "Does 'everyone' have to know?" they wonder. No: Privacy is protected by federal laws. Health-insurance privacy protection is provided by the federal privacy laws HIPAA and 42 CFR Part 2 (which is specific to substance-use privacy protection).

LOCATING APPROPRIATE CARE

When choosing a treatment program, ask specific questions to find out if the program uses practices supported by research. Find out if the program follows the latest scientific knowledge, uses credentialed mental-health and eating disorder treatment professionals, and prescribes medication, when necessary, to assist in the recovery process.

If the program follows evidence-based practices, you will have a better chance of having effective care and improved chances for recovery.

NEDA provides this summary of what treatment is recommended for which severity of diagnosis. Patients who can show that these treatments are needed and provided may persuade insurance companies to pay for them.

Criteria for level of care. Inpatient hospital treatment is called for when a patient is "medically unstable," that is, with unstable or abnormal vital signs (pulse, respiration, and blood pressure, for instance), when lab results show acute risk, or when coexisting medical problems such as diabetes present dangerous complications. They also recommend inpatient treatment when someone is psychiatrically unstable, whether he is suicidal and personally unsafe, or his mental symptoms are rapidly worsening.

Residential treatment—that is, in a nonhospital but live-in facility— is considered appropriate when a patient is medically stable (and so does not require intensive medical interventions) but may be unable to maintain safety without 24-hour supervision to decrease the risk of relapse, and is not considered safe to be at a day treatment facility where he goes home at night.

Many people with eating disorders can benefit from "partial hospital" or day medical treatment. This is appropriate when medical professionals determine that patients are medically stable, that is, their eating disorder may impair functioning without causing immediate acute risk, but they need daily assessment of physiological and mental status.

The least intensive level of care takes place in an outpatient setting. The patients are medically and psychiatrically stable, with symptoms in sufficient control to be able to function in normal social, educational, or vocational situations.

Ideally, a person with an eating disorder should be able to get exactly the level of medical care he or she needs, but often people need to piece together the care they can afford. Campaigns continue for efforts to pass bills requiring better coverage for mental-health conditions, and you'll find suggestions in the next chapter for joining those campaigns.

In an ideal world, eating-disorder treatments would be fully covered. It may seem unfair that they are not. But someone with an eating disorder needs treatment, covered or not. Here are ways to find it.

Lower-cost alternatives. Treatment programs that help people with no money or benefits? Some agencies that receive public funds are required to provide some mental-health care. To find more mental health information, contact:

National Mental Health Information Center
P.O. Box 42557
Washington, DC 20015
(800) 789-2647
(866) 889-2647 (TDD)
nmhic-info@samhsa.hhs.gov
http://mentalhealth.samhsa.gov
Various community agencies may provide free or low-cost treatment. These include family service centers or hospitals with clinics in major cities. They may not specialize in eating disorders, but they can help and they may provide referrals to other resources. For information about community mental-health centers, contact:

National Council for Community Behavioral Health Care
12300 Twinbrook Parkway, Suite 320
Rockville, MD 20852
(301) 984-6200
(301) 881-7159 (fax)
http://www.nccbh.org

On campus. Most colleges have student mental-health centers, or at least specialists, to help students deal with eating disorders, as this is not an unusual issue in college. Groups may be available for treatment and support. Student health-service fees pay for this.

Also, many departments of psychiatry within medical schools have low-fee clinics run by doctors who are being trained as psychiatrists. Even if you are not a student on the campus, you may be eligible for care there. Call the Department of Psychiatry within the medical school and ask if it will accept a patient with an eating disorder. Inquire about sliding-scale fees and ask directly about what type of supervision the residents have available to them.

Research programs and clinical trials. Sometimes treatment can be obtained in the context of a research program. Look for one at a college near you by checking the Treatment Referrals section of NEDA's Web site or by searching for "Eating Disorders" on the U.S. National Institutes of Health's Clinical Trials Web site (http://www. ClinicalTrials.gov).

SELF-HELP GROUPS

Serious cases of eating disorders require serious treatment. But self-help can be a beginning, as it may help to feel in control.

Increase Your Chances for Insurance Coverage

Do your "homework" on what is covered for eating-disorder treatment under your insurance policy and what your state's mandated coverage is, put it in writing, and keep copies of your bills and claims forms. Be ready to appeal denials and check with your state's insurance commission for the "overturn of denial rate." Ask your doctor if he could appeal a denial if you have documented that you meet "medical necessity." Ask your insurance company for a copy of its criteria; many publish their criteria and a number of them have made them available online.

Self-help and support groups are often useful, but they need to be picked with care to make the most of the best of them and avoid the pitfalls. NEDA suggests asking the following questions to help you decide if the self-help group is likely to help you.

1. Does the facilitator or the leader of the group encourage you to seek professional treatment as well as a self-help group?
2. Are most of the people in the self-help group also in treatment with professionals?
3. Does much of the discussion revolve around exchange of information? For example, does the group bring in speakers that teach about some of the consequences of semi-starvation and how to decrease these complications?
4. Is there a central theme that maintaining a healthy body weight is the goal?
5. Does the group avoid simplistic or faddish ideas about how to recover?
6. Does the group talk about common problems and try to solve them?
7. Does the group avoid exchanging information about "how to purge" or "how to diet"?
8. Are members of the group actually improving in terms of normalizing their eating patterns and decreasing purge behavior?
9. Do you have a sense of support and belonging when you go to the group?

If the answers are "yes" to all or most of these questions, the group may be of benefit.

Find an eating-disorder support group. Find an eating-disorder support group in your area, whether you struggle with anorexia, bulimia, binge-eating disorder, or related problems. Here are referral sources for eating disorder support groups.

National Association of Anorexia Nervosa and Related Disorders (ANAD)
http://anad.org/5106/index.html
ANAD does not provide specific information on groups on its site, but you can contact the association for help in finding a group. Submit a request for information about groups near you. ANAD requires you to provide your name, address, and e-mail address, which are kept confidential, and allows space for you to make

special requests. You can also call the ANAD Hotline, 9 A.M. to 5 P.M., Monday through Friday, at (847) 831-3438. Or e-mail ANAD at anad20@aol.com.

Eating Disorders Anonymous (EDA)
http://www.eatingdisordersanonymous.org
Reference for locating 12-step groups focused on eating disorders. Eating Disorders Anonymous groups seek to achieve balance for those who attend, avoiding rigidity.

EDReferral.com
http://edreferral.com/easy_search.htm
Lists all support groups in its database on a single page, organized by state. Descriptions of each group are helpful.

National Eating Disorders Association (NEDA)
http://www.nationaleatingdisorders.org/p.asp?WebPage_ID = 497
This page allows you to search by state and is specific to support groups. Lots of entries are in this database.

Overeaters Anonymous (OA)
http://www.oa.org
Reference for finding 12-step groups dedicated to addressing compulsive overeating. Those who attend will be encouraged to develop an eating plan with a professional.

Pale Reflections Treatment Finder
http://www.pale-reflections.com/treatment_finder.asp
Most entries in this searchable database are therapists and treatment centers. A few support groups are listed.

Something Fishy's Treatment Finder
http://www.somethingfishy.org/treatmentfinder
Something Fishy is an eating disorder support site. Hint: In the "For" box on the treatment finder page, scroll down and select "support groups" to narrow your search. Some providers of group therapy will pop up as well.

WHAT YOU NEED TO KNOW
- Treatment is available but can be costly.
- Insurance and public financial support may be available.
- Professional support is needed and may guide you to other sources for additional support.

11

Preventing Eating Disorders

As you've learned, eating disorders are complicated conditions that are difficult to diagnose and treat. Anorexia, bulimia, and the other related disorders affect not only the people who have them, but their families and friends as well. They can be more difficult to recover from given today's ever-present social and cultural messages of "Eat! Eat! Eat!" and "Diet! Diet! Diet!"

One way to avoid the pain and damage caused by eating disorders is to prevent them. Now that you know some of the facts about eating disorders, you can help to prevent them, in yourself, in your friends and family, and even in your community.

The risk of developing an eating disorder can be reduced in several ways. Individuals can be helped to avoid them, through education and support, developing the positive aspects of a young person's life and future. Or, once the disorders start, they can be cut short before they become ingrained and long-term by early and effective treatment. In society as a whole, eating disorders can be prevented by education and information. Treated as diseases, they can be prevented as a disease through research.

The process for making any kind of change involves first being aware of the problem: acknowledging that something is wrong. Then a person or society has to want to make a change. Change can occur when an individual or a society takes action. So, whether you are dealing with an eating disorder on your own or in a friend—or trying to make a difference on a wider scale—you can help gather information and work for change.

Being aware of the dangers and symptoms of eating disorders, you can help yourself and others want to make positive change—and here are some suggested actions for making those changes.

With the information you have now, take a new look at your own eating and exercise patterns. Do you fit any of the patterns described in earlier chapters? If you've noticed that some of the items in those checklists seem familiar, think about taking some steps toward new behaviors.

And do you feel good about yourself? Find something to do that does make yourself feel good about who you are, not about what you think you look like.

While you're at it, see how some of your best friends answer those questions.

Take a look around your home and family. Do you notice that your parent or older siblings are saying "I'm fat," or forcing themselves to overexercise or practicing "yo-yo" dieting? Do you hear more praise for how you look or dress than for all the interesting things you do? Do you ever feel like what you do is "never enough," that your sports achievements or club activities or grades could be just a little more or better? Do you watch a family member restrict his eating or overdo his exercise? If so, try to talk with your family about it. If you find that hard, show them this book or get information from some of the sources listed in the back and share that with them.

It can be tricky for parents, figuring out the best for their children's health and self-esteem at a time when there is a great deal of social concern about obesity, and significant pressure to do well. Many parents worry about how to get their kids a healthy diet, and prevent them from becoming obese or overweight without giving them anxiety about food that might lead to an eating disorder. The best thing to do is to emphasize health rather than their weight.

What's needed is an overall healthy lifestyle for you and your family. Just as it's important to eat from all the food groups, it's important to engage in a balanced variety of activities. Does your little brother spend all his time with his electronic games? Is your sister at the computer for hours? Exercise and positive activities are as important as eating well for building a healthy life. Think of some small changes that your family might make to develop more fun and energy. Help with the cooking and shopping! And remember: It's okay to eat when you're hungry, and refuse food when you're not. It's okay to exercise because it's fun, not because it's a demand.

TO PARENTS AND TEACHERS

Parents may feel guilty and ashamed when children develop eating disorders, but that may not be helpful. Rather, take positive actions: First, be aware enough of the conditions that you recognize them. Don't try to hide from them, but instead use these tips for preventing eating disorders in the children and teens in your life, as suggested by ANRED and other experts.

> ➤ Model behavior for your kids and teens. "Do as I do" is the best rule in setting good eating patterns—adults who don't diet, don't tease, and don't allow that behavior in their homes are more likely to have kids who are comfortable with their healthy selves.
> ➤ Encourage health habits of eating and exercising.
> ➤ Praise fitness, not thinness; personality, not looks—in your kids, their friends, your friends.
> ➤ Don't forbid certain foods; encourage food variety. Encourage fun activity.
> ➤ Have fun—not fights—at mealtime.
> ➤ Help kids interpret media messages: What's real and what's not?
> ➤ Get help when needed. If a kid insists on a diet, insist on healthy nutrition, perhaps with professional guidance.

CUTTING DISORDERS SHORT

What if you see patterns and behavior in your family and friends (or yourself) that give hints of disordered eating or exercise? They may be stopped before they become ingrained and long term. Again, it's about intervention and self-esteem. Think of ways to share the facts you've learned, and take the attitude that people with hints of eating disorders may not feel good about themselves. You can take the action of giving them support.

Take another look at the examples from chapter 1. How would you help these people get back in balance if they were your friends or family members? Can you think of people in your own life who have situations like these?

1. Mary, who wants to lose weight to fit into a prom dress. Make sure she stops dieting after the dance!
2. Lester, whose parents are both overweight. Encourage him to join you in some energetic activities.

3. Alf, who exercises four hours a day. Give him some info about exercise disorders and males.
4. Sonya, who always has to wear the latest style in tiny sizes, but who eats a lot. Pay attention to whether she "disappears" after meals—and share a printout on bulimia.
5. Sally, who is getting skinnier and skinnier, but telling everyone that she's fine. Let her know you care about her (and see more ideas in chapter 9).
6. Stan, who has been a picky eater since babyhood. See if what he does eat is a good mix—and take him along on snack runs!
7. Angelina, whose dream is to be a ballet dancer. Admire her energy and be sure she's fueling it well.
8. Laura, who already smokes a pack of cigarettes a day. Invite her to join you in some *healthy* ways to keep her busy.

If you notice a family member or friend with low self-esteem, severe dieting, and dissatisfaction with appearance, consider talking to them about these issues. Although you may not be able to prevent an eating disorder from developing, you can talk about healthier behavior or treatment options.

PREVENTION IN THE WIDER SOCIETY

What can you do to change a culture? Start by being aware of the negative influences all around you. For instance, take a look at the magazines in your favorite store. Notice the topics listed on the cover: How often do they promise quick tips for weight loss (or bodybuilding)? And notice how often those same covers promote recipes for desserts or have pictures of cakes on the cover. When you're watching TV, count the ads for "magic" weight loss products and gadgets—while you and your friends are at the same time encouraged to sit there at the TV instead of being outside getting exercise! While you're online with your friends or surfing the Internet, be alert to sites or conversations that are misleading about weight control (especially dangerous are the ones that promote anorexia—warn your friends about them).

And then what can you do? Check out the Center for Media Literacy (http://www.medialit.org) and follow its suggestions.

Get involved. The GO GIRLS! program (also for boys) by the National Eating Disorders Association involves high schoolers working together to promote responsible advertising and to advocate for positive body images of youth by the media and major retailers.

Through their participation in the program, GO GIRLS! team members strengthen their personal self-esteem and body image while discovering that they have powerful voices able to effect social, political, and personal change. Participants in this program explore their own body image issues, general principles about eating disorders and prevention, and the connection between media and body image. GO GIRLS! teams take an in-depth look at how advertisements are developed, and, in the process, gain the knowledge to analyze their underlying messages. Team members learn how to construct effective letters and presentations to voice their support or concern to advertisers who either responsibly or irresponsibly impact youth body image.

Tell the government. It's the job of some government agencies to protect people against media messages that are false, misleading, or harmful. If you've got a problem, contact them. To complain about false or misleading advertising:

Federal Trade Commission
CRC-240
600 Pennsylvania Ave NW
Washington, DC 20580
(877) FTC-HELP
http://www.ftc.gov

Preventing discrimination. In addition to fighting for coverage for an individual's eating disorders, you can be part of campaigns to improve insurance coverage for everyone. Faces and Voices of Recovery works toward that goal. Faces and Voices of Recovery (http://www.facesandvoicesofrecovery.org) is an advocacy group of and for people in recovery from a variety of conditions, including addictions and eating disorders, who share their stories and join in actions to improve conditions and attitude.

The Eating Disorders Coalition for Research, Policy & Action (EDC) is a group of nonprofit organizations, treatment centers, and other organizations whose mission is to advocate at the federal level for eating disorders to be recognized as a public-health priority. Its Family & Friends Action Council (FAC) provides an opportunity to share stories of their family struggles in getting help and coverage for their loved ones. For more information on the EDC's Family & Friends Action Council go to http://www.eatingdisorderscoalition.org/involved/involved.html.

The Anna Westin Foundation (http://www.AnnaWestinFoundation.org) provides an example of one family's battle against an insurance company and additional tips on how to appeal to your insurance

Share the Message

You can share what you've learned, whether you write a letter to the local paper or member of Congress—or just offer to speak to a meeting of Girl Scouts or a church youth group. When you contact anyone like that, here's the message that NEDA suggests:

"Eating disorders are illnesses with a biological basis modified and influenced by emotional and cultural factors. The stigma associated with eating disorders has long kept individuals suffering in silence, inhibited funding for crucial research, and created barriers to treatment. Because of insufficient information, the public and professionals fail to recognize the dangerous consequences of eating disorders. While eating disorders are serious, potentially life-threatening illnesses, there is help available and recovery is possible." Then continue with what you hope to achieve by the letter or article: "But people with eating disorders need your help—with financing, with understanding, with. . . ."

company. Finally, the Patient Advocate Foundation (http://www. patientadvocate.org or [800] 532-5274) provides information and resources, including sample appeals letters and more.

LOOKING AHEAD

When people are in the midst of disordered lifestyles, there often seems no way out, even when they want to change. But people who have been there can share that there is a healthy future ahead.

Personal hopes: What recovery feels like. These are from stories gathered over the years from the Web sites that support recovery. Here's how real young people describe their positive future.

A woman in her early twenties speaks to those who are still struggling with eating disorders:

Though it may be hard to imagine a life without counting calories and purging, I assure you that life is possible for you. We are on this Earth to enjoy ourselves, not hurt ourselves. It's taken me a long time to realize that fact, but once I did, it opened many new doors for me. I am now in recovery, in part because of support. It only takes one true, loyal friend to help you see what life is all about.

Another young woman talks both about the practical issues involved with recovery and the joy that follows:

There is such a better life beyond anorexia and bulimia. Hope can spring from a landscape of bleakness. Joy can take the place of misery. Sadness can become an emotion, not a life sentence. Recovery from anorexia or bulimia is like a mandate to do what everyone else is working not to do. I feel proud every time I eat a box of french fries. I work diligently to incorporate fat into my diet. I am careful not to eat too many fruits and vegetables. Artificial sweetener tops my list of foods not to eat. Fat tops my list of foods to eat. Eating has become such a minor part of my life. No more agony, no more fear. And I love my body. It is a beautiful thing—the product of millions of years of evolution, and a repository of the genes of my family. I have energy to do amazing things with this body of mine. But even more importantly, I am happy, content, energetic, hopeful, and can think about someone besides myself. I am actually *fun* to be around. I think the thing I was most afraid of when I went into therapy was that they would fix my eating disorder, but I would still be miserable. But you can fix it all!! You can be happy. Most people are not depressed. Most people never think about killing themselves. Most people are happy a lot of the time. People with depression can be like most people if they seek treatment.

A teen reports:

I haven't vomited in over two and a half years. I haven't wanted to in probably two years. I haven't restricted my eating in at least as long. I take antidepressants, and under my doctor's supervision, I am slowly reducing the dosage. I still get sad, but it goes away. I sometimes worry about my weight, but it passes. My life is better than I could have imagined. I have everything that I thought that losing weight would bring me and more—at a healthy weight. And I look a hell of a lot better!!

One girl tells about the lesser-known benefits of recovery:

My hair is incredibly shiny. It is also thicker and grows more quickly. My sores heal more quickly—including acne, which I have less of. My eyes are shiny and full of life. I am much stronger. I'm not too hot or too cold all of the time. I have all kinds of time that I never seemed to have before. I can just sit and do nothing (and not think about food at the same time!).

Is it worth it, to work so hard to give up something that has been at the core of one's life? Here are some final words from some members of a recovery support group:

To anyone in recovery, please know that it is so possible to be free! But it is a lot of work and there are so many things that will go through your head that you won't believe about yourself. But they are true; you are a great person and nothing or no one can make you feel like less than anyone else unless you give them permission to do so. Give yourself permission to ditch your rules and make new ones where YOU are the deserving one, because, at last, we do deserve to be happy.

My advice to all girls with eating disorders: Food is not an enemy; you must have it or you will die. You use up at least 1,000 calories a day at rest! Look at a height-weight chart. Most likely, you are underweight. Weight is needed to live! And if you have what you need, you will look and feel great! I enjoy chicken, steak, rice, yogurt, and low-fat treats and haven't gained an ounce from them! You can, too! Realize that life is not about what you look like, it is about being happy. And believe me, being underweight does not make you happy! You only have one life: You can waste it or use it to the fullest. Learn to eat real food; God gave it to us to do just that!

Research hopes. Serious research into the causes of and treatments for eating disorders is a recent scientific effort. With 21st-century tools for studying the body and the brain, government agencies and private groups are exploring effective ways to prevent and stop the damage of eating disorders. A wide range of research is contributing to advances in the understanding and treatment of eating disorders. For instance, the federal government sponsors many research projects. NIMH-funded scientists and others continue to investigate the effectiveness of psychosocial interventions, medications, and the combination of these treatments with the goal of improving outcomes for people with eating disorders.

Other federal research on interrupting the binge-eating cycle has shown that once a structured pattern of eating is established, the person experiences less hunger, less deprivation, and a reduction in negative feelings about food and eating. The two factors that increase the likelihood of bingeing—hunger and negative feelings—are reduced, which decreases the frequency of binges. Several family and twin studies suggest a genetic vulnerability to developing anorexia and bulimia. Scientists suspect that multiple genes may interact with environmental and other factors to increase the risk of developing these illnesses. The more closely they can identify the sources, the greater the possibility of improved treatments for eating disorders.

Other studies are investigating the neurobiology of emotional and social behavior relevant to eating disorders and the neuroscience of feeding behavior. That is, they are studying the connection between neurotransmitters and eating patterns. Scientists have learned that both appetite and energy expenditure are regulated by a highly complex network of nerve cells and molecular messengers called neuropeptides, and future discoveries may provide potential targets for the development of new pharmacologic treatments for eating disorders.

Some potentially valuable insights are likely to come from studying the role of reproductive hormones, since these disorders usually begin around puberty. You can read the most up to date information about research at the U.S. National Institutes of Health Web site (http://www.nimh.nih.gov/healthinformation).

Prospects for pharmaceutical treatments. Studies reported in the *Archives of General Psychiatry* suggest that a drop in brain levels of the neurotransmitter serotonin and its precursor, tryptophan, may

Check This Out

Here are more actions you can take:

Ask your school for active recess.

Ask your school to remove candy machines from school.

Find out how many calories you need each day.

Look at the lunch at your school: Is it balanced?

Maybe do a project on one of these topics and write a report on it for class or the school newspaper.

trigger symptoms of the eating disorder bulimia nervosa in vulnerable individuals. It works like this: Healthy adult females who diet may experience a reduction in brain serotonin, which then may trigger the cycle of bingeing and purging. Scientists hope that pinpointing the exact nature of serotonin's relationship to eating disorders as well as other possible biological underpinnings may lead to more successful treatment methods.

The accumulating research is leading to an increased understanding of how brain chemicals influence eating and behavior. This knowledge may help develop new techniques for diagnosing eating disorders. These new diagnostic tools may, in turn, help develop new methods to treat eating disorders.

MOVING AHEAD TO A POSITIVE FUTURE

Serious research has begun only relatively recently, and it has come a long way quickly.

People suffering from eating disorders need to know that a healthy future is close by, right on the "other side" if they are just willing to reach for it. In the same way, families and professionals who must deal with eating disorders need to remember that sooner rather than later solutions are possible.

WHAT YOU NEED TO KNOW

> ▸ Eating disorders can be treated in various ways and at various stages.
> ▸ Individuals can be helped to avoid them, with professional guidance and personal support.
> ▸ Outcomes can be improved with early intensive intervention.
> ▸ They can be reduced in society as a whole by education and information, and there are groups to join for united action.
> ▸ They can be prevented as a disease through research, which is continuing on public and private fronts.
> ▸ Sharing research information can help improve outcomes.

APPENDIX

Helpful Organizations and Web Sites

The groups listed here are excellent sources for information, help, and referrals. These Web sites are factual and nonpromotional.

In case of immediate emergency, dial 911.

About-Face
P.O. Box 77665
San Francisco, CA 94107
(415) 436-0212
http://www.about-face.org
About-Face says its mission is to equip women and girls with tools to understand and resist the harmful stereotypes of women the media disseminates. There are three components to the About-Face program "Education into Action": media-literacy workshops, action groups, and this resource-filled Web site. About-Face is based in San Francisco, California. Its workshops and action groups reach throughout the San Francisco Bay Area.

Academy for Eating Disorders (AED)
111 Deer Lake Road, Suite 100
Deerfield, IL 60015
(847) 498-4274
info@aedweb.org
http://www.aedweb.org
The Academy for Eating Disorders describes itself as a global, multidisciplinary professional organization that provides cutting-edge professional training and education, inspires new developments in eating-disorders research, prevention, and clinical treatments, and serves as an international source for advocacy and state-of-the-art information to professionals and the public in the field of eating disorders.

American Academy of Child and Adolescent Psychiatry (AACAP)
3615 Wisconsin Avenue NW

Washington, DC 20016-3007
(202) 966-7300
http://www.aacap.org
Visit the AACAP Web site for information on finding a psychiatrist in your area.

American Dietetic Association (ADA)

6 West Jackson Boulevard
Chicago, IL 60606
(800) 877-1600
http://www.eatright.org
The ADA can provide thorough information about good nutrition as well as contacts to professionals who can provide help for possible eating disorders.

American Psychiatric Association

1000 Wilson Boulevard, Suite 1825
Arlington, VA 22209
(888) 357-7924
http://www.psych.org
Contact the APA Answer Center at (888) 357-7924 for information about the APA's services, programs, and activities.

American Psychological Association

750 First Street NE
Washington, DC 20002
(800) 374-2721
http://www.apa.org
The American Psychological Association provides information about various aspects of psychological and emotional disorders, and can provide a referral to a specialist in your area at (800) 964-2000.

ANAD, National Association of Anorexia Nervosa and Associated Eating Disorders

P.O. Box 7
Highland Park, IL 60035
(847) 831-3438
http://www.anad.org
ANAD focuses on advocacy and education but also provides hotline services, group support, and referrals, at no charge. ANAD sponsors over 350 groups in the United States and in 18 foreign countries.

Anna Westin Foundation
http://www.AnnaWestinFoundation.org
*Provides an example of one family's battle against an insurance
company and additional tips on how to appeal to your insurance
company.*

Eating Disorders Coalition for Research, Policy and Action (EDC)
611 Pennsylvania Avenue SE, #423
Washington, DC 20003-4303
(202) 543-9570
http://www.eatingdisorderscoalition.org
*EDC is a group of nonprofit organizations, treatment centers, and
other organizations whose mission is to advocate at the federal
level for eating disorders to be recognized as a public-health
priority. Its Family & Friends Action Council (FAC) provides an
opportunity to share stories of their family struggles in getting help
and coverage for their loved ones.*

Eating Disorders Referral and Information Center
2923 Sandy Pointe, Suite 6
Del Mar, CA 92014
http://www.edreferral.com
*EDReferral's Web site provides information and treatment resources
for all forms of eating disorders.*

National Eating Disorders Association (NEDA)
603 Stewart Street, Suite 803
Seattle, WA 98101
(800) 931-2237
info@NationalEatingDisorders.org
http://www.nationaleatingdisorders.org
*The National Eating Disorders Association is the largest nonprofit
organization in the United States working to eliminate eating
disorders. It incorporates other groups, including Eating Disorders Awareness & Prevention (EDAP), the American Anorexia
Bulimia Association (AABA), the National Eating Disorder
Organization (NEDO), and Anorexia Nervosa & Related Disorders (ANRED). The combined focus of these groups is to expand
public understanding of eating disorders and also to promote
access to quality treatment for those affected along with support
for their families through education, advocacy, and research.
Its Web site offers thorough information and links to other
resources.*

Mental Health America
2000 N. Beauregard Street, 6th Floor
Alexandria, VA 22311
(800) 273-TALK
Formerly the National Association of Mental Health, MHA provides information about symptoms and treatment for a full range of mental illnesses, including eating disorders.

National Alliance on Mental Illness (NAMI)
Colonial Place Three
2107 Wilson Boulevard, Suite 300
Arlington, VA 22201-3042
(800) 950-6264
http://www.nami.org
NAMI is the nation's largest grassroots mental health organization dedicated to improving the lives of persons living with serious mental illness and their families.

National Institute of Mental Health
6001 Executive Boulevard, Room 8184
MSC 9663
Bethesda, MD 20892-9663
(866) 615-6464
nimhinfo@nih.gov
http://www.nimh.nih.gov/publicat/eatingdisorders.cfm
The National Institute of Mental Health (NIMH), a federal agency, is the largest scientific organization in the world dedicated to research focused on the understanding, treatment, and prevention of mental disorders and the promotion of mental health.

Overeaters Anonymous (OA)
World Service Office
P.O. Box 44020
Rio Rancho, NM 87174-4020
(505) 891-2664
info@oa.org
http://www.oa.org
OA is a nonprofit international organization of volunteer support groups modeled after the 12-step Alcoholics Anonymous program. The OA recovery program of mutual self-help addresses physical, emotional, and spiritual recovery aspects of compulsive overeating, and addresses other eating disorders. Members are encouraged to

seek professional help for individual nutrition assistance and for any emotional or physical problems.

Patient Advocate Foundation
(800) 532-5274
http://www.patientadvocate.org
Provides information and resources for help with medical coverage, including sample appeal letters and more.

Screening for Mental Health, Inc. (SMH)
One Washington Street, Suite 304
Wellesley, MA 02481-1706
(781) 239-0071
http://www.mentalhealthscreening.org
SMH is a nonprofit organization that coordinates mental-health screening programs nationwide, including the National Eating Disorders Screening Program (NEDSP), a large-scale screening for eating disorders, and interactive telephone screening programs. The screening programs include an educational presentation on eating disorders, body image, and nutrition, as well as a written test and the opportunity to meet one-on-one with a health professional.

Social Security Administration
(800) 772-1213
http://ssa.gov
For information about benefits from Social Security, Medicare, and disability benefits, call the U.S. Social Security Administration. For information about Medicaid, contact your local social service or welfare office. You can also find information about Medicare and Medicaid at the Centers for Medicare & Medicaid Services (http://www.cms.gov).

GLOSSARY

addiction   Irresistible physiological and/or psychological need for a habit-forming substance or behavior.

amenorrhea   Absence of menstrual periods; can occur in ANOREXIA.

anorexia nervosa   An EATING DISORDER characterized by refusal to maintain normal body weight; intense fear of gaining weight; body-image distortion; and AMENORRHEA. There are two types: restricting, which involves self-starvation without bingeing or purging; and binge-eating/purging, where BINGES or PURGES are added to dieting.

anxiety disorders   Mental disorders marked by physiological arousal, feelings of tension, and intense apprehension without apparent reason. Can be either a trigger or a result of eating disorders.

athletica nervosa   Compulsive overexercising.

behavioral psychology   A form of psychotherapy that uses basic learning techniques to modify maladaptive behavior patterns by substituting new responses to given stimuli for undesirable ones.

bigorexia   An obsession with becoming big and muscular, often as a way to compensate for perceived physical inadequacies. More prevalent among boys and men.

binge eating   The consumption of an unusually large quantity of high-calorie food within a brief period of time. It can occur within the context of any eating disorder, as well as in nonpathological situations.

binge-eating disorder (BED)   An EATING DISORDER characterized by recurrent episodes of bingeing—that is, eating large quantities of food more rapidly than normal, until uncomfortably full, and when not hungry. Bingeing episodes cause distress and are not followed by any type of PURGE.

body dysmorphic disorder (BDD)   An excessive preoccupation with some minor flaw or imagined defect in physical appearance. Someone with BDD has problems controlling negative thoughts about appearance, even when told by others that they look fine.

bulimarexia   A combination of BULIMIA and ANOREXIA: An EATING DISORDER in which one alternates between abnormal craving for

126

and aversion to food. It is characterized by episodes of excessive food intake followed by periods of fasting and self-induced vomiting or diarrhea.

bulimia nervosa Eating disorder characterized by recurrent episodes of bingeing followed by compensatory behavior to prevent weight gain; e.g., vomiting, use of LAXATIVES, DIURETICS, enemas, or excessive exercise.

calorie Quantity of heat required to raise the temperature of one gram of water by 1 °C from a standard initial temperature; a unit of energy contained in food, as measured by burning food in a calorimeter.

cognitive behavioral therapy (CBT) A form of psychological therapy that focuses on an individual's ability to learn new behaviors.

compulsion An irresistible impulse to commit an irrational act. Compulsive overeating, for example, indicates people who use food to manage stress and uncomfortable emotions, and overeat in spite of their fears about gaining weight.

cortisol A corticosteroid hormone produced by the adrenal gland that increases blood pressure and reduces immune responses. Often called the *stress hormone* because it becomes increased in response to stress. It can cause elevated blood pressure and blood sugar.

dialectical behavioral therapy (DBT) A psychological treatment method that involves both individual meetings between therapist and patient (where behavioral skills are learned) and group meetings (where participants learn more about using those skills).

dieting Avoiding eating certain types of food (craving may lead to bingeing); or restricting the total amount of food eaten (starving, which may lead to bingeing).

dehydration Decreased fluid in the body, which may result in feelings of dizziness and weakness accompanied by low blood pressure and fast heart rate. When prolonged, it can cause serious physical damage and/or death.

denial A psychological term for refusing to acknowledge the facts.

diuretic A substance or drug that tends to increase the discharge of urine; may be used by people with EATING DISORDERS in the mistaken belief that it prevents weight gain. As with LAXATIVES, individuals may feel they've lost weight because of the resulting DEHYDRATION. Abuse of diuretics can easily result in depletion of important ELECTROLYTES, such as sodium and potassium.

eating disorder not otherwise specified (EDNOS) Disordered food-related patterns that do not fit standard diagnoses—for example, the pattern of chewing and spitting out large amounts of food without swallowing.

eating disorders   Any of several psychological disorders relating to the consumption of food, such as ANOREXIA NERVOSA and BULIMIA. They are characterized by an abnormal fear of obesity, distorted body image, and subsequent abnormal eating patterns.

electrolytes   Electrical conductors in which current is carried by ions, as in the body. Their function is to communicate nerve messages throughout all the systems of the body. DEHYDRATION and/or loss of electrolytes like sodium can result in lethargy and weakness; low potassium can lead to heart problems and weakness in other muscles.

emetic   A substance that causes vomiting.

endorphins   Any of a group of neurotransmitters that affect mood, perception of pain, memory retention, and learning. Their appropriate chemical makeup requires the ingestion of a balanced diet.

enema   The procedure of introducing liquids into the rectum and colon through the anus as a way of inducing a bowel movement.

family therapy   A form of psychotherapy in which the interrelationships of family members are examined in group sessions in order to identify and alleviate the problems of one or more members of the family.

hormones   Chemicals released in the body by exocrine or endocrine glands whose action may regulate tissues and organs. Inadequate nutrition may affect adequate production of hormones—for example, as the production of the hormone estrogen affects bone density.

insight therapies   Therapy techniques based on the assumption that a person's behavior, thoughts, and emotions can be changed or influenced by understanding what motivates him or her. Cognitive behavior therapy (CBT) is one type of insight therapy.

lanugo   Very fine white hair that sometimes grows on the arms and chest (or other parts of the body) of girls with anorexia who are severely emaciated.

laxative   A food or drug that causes looseness or evacuation of the bowels; may be used by people who have EATING DISORDERS to purge food from the body in an attempt to avoid caloric absorption.

Maudsley method   An approach to anorexia treatment that involves the parents. Initially, parents are temporarily placed in charge of their child's eating behaviors. As the child approaches target weight, he or she is rewarded with increased control over their own eating.

medical nutrition therapy   The use of specific nutrition services to treat an illness, injury, or condition. It includes diet therapy, counseling, or use of specialized nutrition supplements.

metabolism   The interaction of physical and chemical processes occurring within a living cell or organism that are necessary for the maintenance of life. In human metabolism substances derived from food are broken down into basic substances to yield energy both for activity and for vital organic processes.

neuroendocrine system   Of, relating to, or involving the interaction between the nervous system and the HORMONES of the endocrine glands.

neuropeptide   Any of a variety of chemical messengers released by the brain. Neuropeptides are responsible for many physical and emotional functions including mood, energy levels, and body weight.

obsession   Compulsive preoccupation with a fixed idea or an unwanted feeling or emotion, often accompanied by symptoms of anxiety; also, an intense, often unreasonable idea or emotion.

obsessive-compulsive behaviors   A pattern of preoccupation with perfectionism, and mental and interpersonal control, at the expense of flexibility, openness, and efficiency. EATING DISORDERS may involve both an obsession (a thought pattern) and a compulsion (a behavior pattern).

orthorexia   The OBSESSION to eat only foods that are healthy and/or organic.

psychonutritional therapy   An approach to the treatment of EATING DISORDERS in which psychotherapy and MEDICAL NUTRITION THERAPY carry through the entire recovery process.

psychopharmacology   An area of psychiatry that deals with the study of the actions and effects of psychoactive drugs and their application. Eating-disorder therapy may involve the use of psychoactive drugs, especially where other conditions such as depression are present.

purge   To cause emptying of, as the bowels or other segments of the digestive tract; in EATING DISORDERS through the use of LAXATIVES, EMETICS, or self-induced vomiting.

rational emotive behavioral therapy (REBT or EBT)   A form of COGNITIVE BEHAVIORAL THERAPY that focuses on actively connecting thoughts and feelings toward changing behaviors.

serotonin   A neurotransmitter that affects emotional states among other functions. Thought to be related to the physiological processes of EATING DISORDERS.

water loading   The practice of drinking excessive amounts of water prior to a weight-in, in order to give a false high reading of weight.

READ MORE ABOUT IT

Andersen, Arnold, Leigh Cohn, and Thomas Holbrook. *Making Weight: Men's Conflicts with Food, Weight, Shape and Appearance.* Carlsbad, Calif.: Gürze Books, 2000.

Becker, Daniel. *This Mean Disease: Growing Up in the Shadow of My Mother's Anorexia.* Carlsbad, Calif.: Gürze Books, 2005.

Brashich, Audrey. *All Made Up: A Girl's Guide to Seeing Through Celebrity Hype.* Carlsbad, Calif.: Gürze Books, 2007.

Bruch, Hilde. *Eating Disorders: Obesity, Anorexia Nervosa, and the Person Within.* New York: Basic Books, 1973.

———. *The Golden Cage: The Enigma of Anorexia Nervosa.* Cambridge, Mass.: Harvard University Press, 1978.

Chernin, Kim. *The Hungry Self: Women, Eating, and Identity.* New York: Harper & Row, 1985.

Costin, Carolyn. *Eating Disorders Source Book.* Los Angeles: Lowell House, 1999.

———. *100 Questions and Answers about Eating Disorders.* Carlsbad, Calif.: Gürze Books, 2006.

Davis, Brangien. *What's Real, What's Ideal: Overcoming a Negative Body Image.* New York: Rosen Publishing Group, 1998.

Dellasega, Cheryl. *The Starving Family: Caregiving Mothers and Fathers Share Their Eating Disorder Wisdom.* Fredonia, Wis.: Champion Press, 2005.

Friedman, Sandra. *When Girls Feel Fat: Helping Girls through Adolescence.* New York: HarperCollins, 1998.

Friend, Natasha. *Perfect.* Carlsbad, Calif.: Gürze Books, 2004.

Gaesser, Glenn. *Big Fat Lies: The Truth about Your Weight and Your Health.* Carlsbad, Calif.: Gürze Books, 2002.

Garner, David M., and Paul E. Garfinkel, eds. *Handbook of Treatment for Eating Disorders.* New York: Guilford Press, 1997.

Gilbert, Sara Dulaney, with Mary C. Commerford. *The Unofficial Guide to Managing Eating Disorders.* Foster City, Calif.: IDG Books, 2000.

Hall, Lindsey, ed. *Full Lives: Women Who Have Freed Themselves from Food and Weight Obsession.* Carlsbad, Calif.: Gürze Books, 1993.

Hall, Lindsey, and Leigh Cohn. *Bulimia: A Guide to Recovery.* Carlsbad, Calif.: Gürze Books, 1998.

Hall, Lindsey, and Monika Ostroff. *Anorexia Nervosa: A Guide to Recovery.* Carlsbad, Calif.: Gürze Books, 1998.

Hall, Liza F. *Perk! The Story of A Teenager With Bulimia.* Carlsbad, Calif.: Gürze Books, 1997.

Herrin, Marcia, and Nancy Matsumoto. *The Parents' Guide to Childhood Eating Disorders.* Carlsbad, Calif.: Gürze Books, 2007.

Lock, James, and Daniel LeGrange. *Help Your Teenager Beat an Eating Disorder.* Carlsbad, Calif.: Gürze Books, 2004.

Kano, Susan. *Making Peace with Food.* New York: Harper & Row, 1989.

Knapp, Caroline. *Appetites: Why Women Want.* New York: Counterpoint Publishers, 2003.

Koenig, Karen. *The Rules of "Normal" Eating: A Commonsense Approach for Dieters, Overeaters, Undereaters, Emotional Eaters, and Everyone in Between!* Carlsbad, Calif.: Gürze Books, 2005.

———. *The Food and Feelings Workbook: A Full Course Meal on Emotional Health.* Carlsbad, Calif.: Gürze Books, 2005.

Kolodny, Nancy. *The Beginners Guide to Eating Disorders Recovery.* Carlsbad, Calif.: Gürze Books, 2004.

Liu, Aimee. *Gaining: The Truth about Life after Eating Disorders.* New York: Warner Books, 2007.

Maine, Margo, and Joe Kelly. *The Body Myth: Adult Women and the Pressure to Be Perfect.* Carlsbad, Calif.: Gürze Books, 2005.

McFarland, Barbara, and Tyeis Baker-Baumann. *Feeding the Empty Heart.* Minneapolis: Hazelden, 1988.

McShane, Johanna Marie, and Tony Paulson. *Why She Feels Fat.* Carlsbad, Calif.: Gürze Books, 2007.

Nash, Joyce, Ph.D. *Binge No More: Your Guide to Overcoming Disordered Eating.* Carlsbad, Calif.: Gürze Books, 1999.

Neumark-Sztainer, Dianne. *"I'm, Like, SO Fat!": Helping Your Teen Make Healthy Choices about Eating and Exercise in a Weight-Obsessed World.* Carlsbad, Calif.: Gürze Books, 2005.

Normandi, Carol Emery, and Laurelee Roark. *Over It: A Teen's Guide to Getting Beyond Obsessions with Food and Weight.* Carlsbad, Calif.: Gürze Books, 2001.

Otis, Carol, and Roger Goldingay. *The Athletic Woman's Survival Guide.* Carlsbad, Calif.: Gürze Books, 2000.

Pipher, Mary. *Reviving Ophelia.* New York: Ballantine Books, 1994.

Roth, Geneen. *When Food Is Love: Exploring the Relationship between Eating and Intimacy.* New York: Plume Books, 1993.

Siegel, Michelle, Judith Brisman, and Margot Weinshel. *Surviving an Eating Disorder: Perspectives and Strategies for Family and Friends.* Carlsbad, Calif.: Gürze Books, 1997.

Sigler, Jamie-Lynn, and Sheryl Berk. *Wise Girl: What I've Learned about Life, Love and Loss.* New York: Pocket Books, 2002.

Smeltzer, Doris, with Andrea Lynn Smeltzer. *Andrea's Voice: Silenced by Bulimia.* Carlsbad, Calif.: Gürze Books, 2006.

Strober, Michael, and Meg Schneider. *Just a Little Too Thin: How to Pull Your Child Back from the Brink of an Eating Disorder.* Carlsbad, Calif.: Gürze Books, 2000.

Walsh, B. Timothy, and Carrie Arnold. *Next to Nothing.* Carlsbad, Calif.: Gürze Books, 2007.

Walsh, David. *Why Do They Act That Way? A Survival Guide to the Adolescent Brain For You and Your Teen.* New York: Free Press/Simon & Schuster, 2004.

Yager, Joel, and Pauline S. Powers, eds. *Clinical Manual of Eating Disorders.* Washington, D.C.: American Psychiatric Publishing, 2007.

Zerbe, Kathryn J. *The Body Betrayed: A Deeper Understanding Of Women, Eating Disorders, and Treatment.* Carlsbad, Calif.: Gürze Books, 1995.

INDEX